£7

HRB

# Three Degrees West

D1142447

# Three Degrees West

## A Walk through Britain's Local and Natural History

STEPHEN SANKEY

With illustrations by
DONALD GUNN

JOHN DONALD PUBLISHERS LTD
EDINBURGH

© Stephen Sankey 1990
All rights reserved. No part of this publication may be reproduced
in any form or by any means without the prior permission of the
publishers, John Donald Publishers Ltd., 138 St. Stephen Street,
Edinburgh EH3 5AA.

ISBN 0 85976 299 8

*British Library Cataloguing in Publication Data*
Sankey, Stephen
    Three degrees west: a walk through Britain's local and
    natural history.
    1. Great Britain. Description & travel
    I. Title
    914.104859

Typeset by Newtext Composition Ltd., Glasgow
Printed by Wheatons Ltd., Exeter

# Acknowledgements

This book could not have been written without the help of many people. Walking in a straight line is not easy! People dropped me off, people picked me up, I stayed over with friends or relatives. To all below I owe my thanks.

*In chronological order:*

Elaine Hammersley; my father, Jack Sankey; my sister, Elaine Mottershaw; Lorna and Richard Jenner; my mother, Angela Flynn; Annette Birch; Ann and Richard Greenwood and family; Bob Metcalfe, Chris Hill, Jo-Jo and Nicky; Elsie and Norman Howe; Bryony Penn; Jim Aitken and Sandra; Robin Callander, Elizabeth Leighton and Rick Worrell; Edward, Richard and Susanna Wade-Martins and Bertrand; Heather, Mike and Thomas Cook; Edwin and Dot Groat; and my grandparents, Eliza and the late Jack Sankey.

Thanks also to June Watson who typed the manuscript; John Tuckwell of John Donald Publishers who picked this ball up and ran; my father for additional photographs (as credited); Dave Miller who printed the photographs; Eric Hayward for the illustration of the Cartmel misericord; and to my friend Donald Gunn, who has captured the wildlife of three degrees with his pencil.

And special thanks to the two beyond chronology, my wife Kate, and my partner for the journey, Meg. I couldn't have made it without you both.

# Author's Note

Walking in the countryside with a dog as a companion gives me enormous pleasure. It should be noted, though, that Meg has been trained to high standards and would, if necessary, walk at heel all day. Wildlife or stock may be stressed or even killed by uncontrolled or poorly trained dogs. For me, walking with a trained dog provides a sixth sense, and rarely have my sightings of wildlife been hindered by Meg. I'm certain that only rats, voles and grey squirrels have come to grief through her on our travels . . . Meg won't even kill rabbits, she'll only push them with her muzzle!

# Contents

**PART I**   **THE SOUTH WEST . . . DORSET, DEVON AND SOMERSET**

1   A FAREWELL TO THE CHANNEL                                          3
The Undercliffs, a wet and wild tangle; snow and Spring;
Downland and hillforts.

2   THE SOMERSET LEVELS                                               11
Dead elms winter the horizon; controversial conservation;
Somerset *withies*.

3   THE PITCHFORK REBELLION                                           17
James, Duke of Monmouth's rising; a crazy lawyer; Meg the
sheepdog; the coast.

**PART II**   **WALES AND THE MARCHES**

4   THE MONMOUTHSHIRE AND BRECON CANAL                                22
The Welsh; saltmarsh perfection; grey Newport; wayward
Glasgow Rangers supporters; a canal-side pitch.

5   OFFA'S DYKE                                                       27
A big dog fox; the Bee of Gwent; Abergavenny; the Celtic
mists of time.

6   ACROSS THE WYE INTO KILVERT COUNTRY                               30
The Black Mountain ridge; Arthur's Stone; an unpleasant
farmer; turnpikes and the Rebecca Riots; toll collectors
and floods.

7   MARCHMEN                                                          35
An old shepherd; lunch with the locals; ridges and mists,
history and buzzards.

8   A SHROPSHIRE LAD                                                  39
King Offa; Owain Glyndwr; Knighton, the town on the dyke;
a lost notebook.

9   THE STIPERSTONES                                                  45
Splendid estate parkland; the Devil's Chair; five lead pigs;
old wood pasture; Shropshire lunarscape.

10  THE SHROPPIE                                              49
    Motte and baileys; in and out of Wales; a jewel of the trip;
    another canal.

11  THE GRESFORD COLLIERY DISASTER                            54
    Chirk aquaduct; Wat's Dyke; coalfield communities.

12  THE WIRRAL                                                60
    Modern man; Estate woodlands; a puppet politician; the
    Manchester Ship Canal.


**PART III**          **THE LANCASHIRE COAST**

13  AINSDALE SANDS                                            66
    A cold, grey wind; asparagus beds; rare reptiles; the Southport
    sanctuary.

14  GOOD OLD BLACKPOOL                                        73
    A toddler is a dunlin; a king and a pretender; a tram ride;
    fish and chips.

15  MEDIEVAL MONKS                                            79
    A rotted carcass; the Scots goose; Cockersand Abbey; Glasson
    dock; the city of Lancaster.


**PART IV**           **THE ENGLISH LAKES**

16  LAKELAND VILLAGES                                         86
    Cartmel Priory; charcoal burners; Grizedale Forest; trouble
    at Hawkshead!

17  HELVELLYN                                                 92
    Grasmere gingerbread; William Wordsworth; Gough and
    his dog; Thirlmere's revenge.

18  BLENCATHRA TO EDEN                                        96
    A domestic dispute; crossing the Caldew; the Border
    City; the Debatable land.

19  THE BORDER CITY                                          101
    A domestic dispute; a tailor's dummy on the Caldew;
    into Carlisle.

**PART V**      **THE SCOTTISH BORDERS**

20   THE QUEEN O' MEG' DALE     106
Gretna Green; the Scotsdike; an encounter with a bull;
Langholm; yellow lava flows.

21   BORDER FORESTS     112
The uplands advance; Ronnie Rose, border forester; giant
chessmen; Meg's displeasure.

22   TRAQUAIR AND TWEED     118
Tramping forest rides; a spooky muir; the historic rivers
of Ettrick, Yarrow and Tweed; a locked gate.

23   GALA WATER     122
A swell of summits; an image of warfare; Gala Water;
Crichton Castle; the clashes of Prestonpans.


**PART VI**      **THE SCOTTISH LOWLANDS**

24   THE ROYAL AND ANCIENT KINGDOM OF FIFE     132
Industrial Fife; Hercules the bear; agricultural Fife; Cupar;
the Tay bridge disaster.

25   DUNDEE AND THE SIDLAWS     141
Jute, jam and journalism; Admiral Duncan and the battle
of Camperdown; over the Sidlaws; Meg stung on the eye;
Glamis Castle; Kirrie.


**PART VII**      **THE SCOTTISH HIGHLANDS**

26   MOUNT KEEN     150
A well kept secret; an aircraft wreck; red deer; conversations
with a keeper; the Queen's Well; the Mounth Road.

27   GROUSE MUIRS     159
Ballater and Victoriana; Caledonian forest; our nemesis;
Grampian characters; the Cabraich.

28   THE SPEYSIDE WAY     167
Dufftown's seven stills; the auld alliance; Fochabers cricket;
Spey salmon.

**PART VIII**     **THE FAR NORTH**

29   THE CAITHNESS COAST                                    174
Wick harbour; Caithness flags; great to be alive; the twin
castles of Sinclair and Girnigoe; the pyramids of the North;
John o'Groats.

30   ORKNEY, THE SLEEPING WHALES                            180
A green and fertile land; a Princess and her dream;
Scapa Flow; the sinking of HMS *Royal Oak*; the Churchill
barriers; an Italian chapel; the city of Kirkwall.

31   MEG SINGS TO THE SELCHIES                              189
A three megawatt windmill; a doocot at Rendall; new friends.

32   THE QUEEN OF THE ISLES AND THE SHIP OF DEATH   192
An archaeological tapestry; ferry loopers; jack snipe and
otter; the Earls of Orkney.

33   ABOARD K440 *THE WINGS OF THE MORNING*                 196
A long day; the dangerous sea; Edwin Groat the skipper;
shooting the creels.

34   THE RETURN OF THE PINKFEET                             201
Westray and its Dons; Meg flies Loganair; the European crane;
a Jacobite cave; the finish, Bow Head.

# Part I    The South West . . . Dorset, Devon and Somerset

Westray Bowhead
Orkney Isles
Kirkwall

Wick
Caithness

Spey Bay

Dufftown
Mount Keen
Grampian
Mountains
Ballater
Kirriemuir

Dundee
SCOTLAND Cupar Methil
The Kingdom
of Fife
Prestonpans

Innerleithen

Scottish Borders
Gretna Green
Carlisle

Keswick
English Lakes

Blackpool
Southport
Liverpool
Eastham
Wrexham

Offa's Dyke
Bishop's Castle Knighton
ENGLAND
Welsh
WALES Marches

Cwmbran Abergavenny
Newport
Weston-super-Mare
Taunton Sedgemoor
Somerset Axminster
Levels Lyme Regis

3°W

Three Degrees West.

# 1     A Farewell to the Channel

## Lyme Regis to Castle Neroche

This book is the story of a wander through Britain with my collie dog Meg. Along the way we encountered a diversity of wildlife, and a wealth of personalities and heritage that only these islands can provide. I spoke to the shepherds of Wales, the keepers of Scotland, the residents of England, and the fishermen of Orkney. I enjoyed the watery plains of the Somerset Levels, the haunting history of Offa's Dyke in the Welsh Marches, the familiarity of my native Lancastrian coastline and the English gem of Lakeland. For some days I traversed my adopted country of Scotland, and wandered the border hills, the royal and ancient Kingdom of Fife, the Grampian mountains and sublime Orkney. On the ancient trackways of Britain wild flowers, birds and animals remain for those who wish to enjoy them in the

The start of three degrees west, Lyme Regis.

quietness of their domain, the backwaters of Britain. And, although our route was subject to daily whims, an essential criterion remained, to follow the line of longitude *three degrees west* of Greenwich, all six hundred miles of it.

Consult a map of Britain, and one finds that the third degree meridian plunges into the English Channel south of Allhallows school in east Devon. We plunged into a tangle of greenery as we descended a country lane and into the jungle of the undercliffs. To make matters worse it was pouring down, and the flint-strewn track was exceedingly slippery. It was the last day of March, and I had not expected such a profuse undergrowth of ivy, mosses, elder and brambles. A camp by the sea seemed an ideal target, but the torn landscape of the landslips rendered this impossible.

The Axmouth–Lyme Regis Undercliffs National Nature Reserve is of great interest since it forms the largest and most important landslip area on the coast of Britain. Exactly why landslips occur is a source of debate, but the key factor is that some ground which is in a saturated state slips away from more consolidated ground. Circumstances such as the angle of slope, the permeability of the rock, the strata and the lines of weakness contained therein, may also have an influence on the scale and form of the slippage. Landslips have occurred here for centuries. Small slips happen most years, and major slips about once a century or so, which have resulted in the confused and chaotic landscape in which I stood. Most of the beds on the site provide fossils, indeed only the marls do not, some of which have wonderful names such as 'tea green marl'. Among the most spectacular fossils are the large ammonites, and removal of these natural trophies is a conservation problem.

Undergrowth and flints gave me little choice of a campsite and resulted in one of the most uncomfortable pitches that I've had. My discomfort caused by the flints epitomised the landslips, since the clay-with-flints layer really belongs to the surface, and several hundred years ago would have been sixty feet or so higher. I finally chose an unsatisfactory location beneath the tall chalk cliffs, praying that the deluge did not provoke a massive landslide equal to the one of Christmas 1839. In this slip, 15 acres of cornfields and hedges slid — some eight million tons of earth — which left a chasm half a mile in length and between 200 and 400 feet in width! Fortunately I discovered this information after my overnight camp in the downpour. The rain had succeeded in soaking the pair of us, and Meg managed to make the inside of the tent as wet as the outside. My sleeping bag was wet through already ... a fine start! During the hours of darkness England had been doing her best to rival our Scottish climate. As I peered from the tent, I was surprised to see that snowflakes had produced a veneer of whiteness. At five-thirty on

Working the oak, Devon.

A tawny owl had
awakened me
*– Undercliffs.*

April 1st, a tawny owl awakened me with its territorial calls of
*kee-wick, kee-wick.* If I strained my ears, I could just hear the sea.
Good enough!

Spring was weeks ahead of Perthshire, and the delightful
yellows of primroses, celandines, hazel catkins and gorse
patterned the greenery with pin-pricks of colour. Fortunately
the snowflakes soon dissolved, to be replaced by stitchwort, the
other snowflakes of the country lanes. We have few incised
tracks lined by ancient hedgerows in Scotland, and to traverse
these lanes in the quietness of spring was pure joy. I walked the
minor roads and tracks whenever possible, for the footpaths in
April are still bogged down in their winter mud which makes for
heavy going.

Edge Hill, north of Allhallows, was an early viewpoint, and I
was feeling good to be away and on the road. Three miles on,
the small town of Axminster was busy with the Sunday morning
hubbub of newspapers, further complicated by Mother's Day
activities. The males of Axminster left the newsagents with
armfuls of daffodils and tabloids and brows heavy with frowns of
responsibility. The church was interesting enough to warrant a
circumnavigation, and amidst yews and gravestones I discovered
the remnants of an overnight drinking binge underneath a
superb Norman arch. I climbed out of Axminster by way of a
long ridge northwards. Looking back over the town, I tried to
imagine the scene of the famous carpet industry which had
begun in 1755. Axminster still lends its name to carpets, but the
industry was transferred to the Wiltshire town of Wilton in the
mid-nineteenth century. According to one source, Axminster

Axminster, alcoholic
arch.

Drake's Farm, Higher
Wambrook.

may be the site of a famous battle of English history, that of
Brunanburh, fought and won by King Athelstan, grandson of
Alfred the Great, over the Irish, Scots and Northumbrian tribes.
It is more likely that this milestone in English history was fought
much further north, nearer to the Viking capital of *Jorvik*
(York). Alfred's grandson became known as 'Glorious Athelstan'
after successfully unifying England, a feat which his grandfather
had embarked upon from his Somerset base of Athelney. King
Athelstan ruled England for fifteen years, but his victory at
Brunanburh in 937, three years before his death, gave a

significant united character to Anglo-Saxon England.

I passed the ancient hillfort of Membury Castle, which had retained its white covering of snow. The downlands were frequented by enormous lowland breeds of sheep. At Bewley Down I was revived by the kindness of Geraldine White, who provided me with a flask of coffee, as I somewhat ungraciously reclined against her sacks of coal. Somewhere nearby I wandered across the county boundary into Somerset. Village after village teased my curiosity. At Wambrook a farmer and his wife proudly informed me that their splendid farmhouse had been built in the 1860s for all of £750, when the settlement belonged to the county of Dorset. Wambrook church was the first of several that I passed with exceedingly tall towers typical of the Somerset perpendicular. Next came Whitestaunton, where I engaged a local farmer in some fun and frolics by photographing his spaniel against a model of some sheep on his wall. Nearby are the remains of a Roman villa in the grounds of the manor-house, and a wood where I slept for a while. Sleeping away the weariness of the road is always a delicious experience.

We crossed the main A303 trunk road, passed the woodland reserve of Dommett Moor, and arrived at my camp at the ancient British fort of Castle Neroche. It is situated on an escarpment overlooking the Somerset Levels, and is such a strategic site that its importance was acknowledged and used by both the Romans and the Normans. Here lies the prospect over Somerset: a prospect over the Levels, dry now, but accustomed to flashes of water reflecting the Polden and Quantock Hills. It's a sweep over Brean Down and the watery access to the Bristol

Fun and frolics, Whitestaunton.

Channel. I even managed to dry out the tent in the early evening sunlight. As I relaxed with my boots off, I watched a pair of nuthatches courting, a rare sight for me, as these colourful birds are not present in Scotland. Something suddenly told me that I was not alone. Meg's hackles rose, then she growled and barked. In the gloom I could make out a figure shuffling in the leaves of the forest floor; the figure seemed brown and tattered, an extension of the earth. Despite the combination of dusk, solitude and Meg's wariness, there seemed no hint of malice in his behaviour, and I did not feel alarmed. I didn't even trouble to leave my cosiness. I concluded that it was a tramp, a professional of the road, and even had pangs of guilt in case I had stolen his retreat. But perhaps the figure was yet more timeless, a Roman camp follower searching for sustenance, or a Norman villager going about his chores? Whatever the explanation I fell soundly asleep!

# 2    The Somerset Levels

## Castle Neroche to Middlezoy

I awoke late at eight to a beautiful day. A keen frost and a chill wind kept me moving smartly on an enjoyable descent through the Neroche plantations, vibrant with the noise of chainsaws and the smell of freshly felled beech. I lost height to discover a rolling countryside of wide old lanes with immense hedgerows. Sheep had predominated on the downlands of yesterday, and these now surrendered to dairy cattle and grain. A pair of buzzards soared over the village of Hatch Beauchamp (pronounced 'Beecham'), where I halted for refreshments. The herd of fallow deer which grazed the parkland of Hatch Court were distinctly pallid in the strong sunlight. Whilst visiting the church I talked with the son of the owner of the Estate, who was occupied in some forestry practice nearby. He lamented the modern housing estates which encroached the village, and spoke fondly of Somerset and Scotland! A coachload of tourists spilled into the Palladian mansion, which is a prominent landmark and had been clearly visible from Neroche on the previous evening.

Back on the road I discovered a badger sett on a laneside. The horizon and ridge ahead, Crimson Hill, was punctuated by dead elms and the chatter of fieldfares, whose pale underwings flashed in the sun as they sped by. Crimson Hill is part of the Currey Rivel ridge above West Sedgemoor:

There is a great roar. And were I not inland, I would think it the sea. A furious blast that is nature's bellows. Some days, not many, are silent.

Stark trees.

Somehow their majestic girths are lost beneath the edge. Even in midsummer, awesome dead elms winter the horizon.

A fierce slope.

Below, the Levels' neat lines parallel the black earth. A far off beast coughs its elegy.

Night falls early.

At dusk I shudder. A fox bark sharpens the cold. And the clatter of woodpigeon and pheasant quicken the heart.

Helicopters droned overhead for most of the morning, and I cursed the noisy intrusions; fighter jets and even monstrous transport planes flew over for good measure. I was obviously in the middle of someone's game. Only when these mechanical noises abated for all too brief a period was it possible to listen to the natural helicopters of the avian world, the skylarks, which were in fine voice. I was informed later during lunch that the activity was caused by the RAF 'training them chaps with things on their heads how to fly'. This rustic Somerset interpretation of events made me smile. My interlocutor was referring to the RAF training of Asian pilots.

Life is full of strange twists, and since beginning this walk, I met a girl who became my wife, who lived at East Lambrook, not five miles off my route to the east. I have come to learn of the honest openness of Somerset folk, who are still bathed in a rural life beyond the lure of London and the Home Counties. They have a passion for cricket and cider which is even reflected in their greetings: 'How's you?' 'Oh . . . rather beyond my guard I'm afraid!'

Lunch at 'The Bird in the Hand' in North Curry was accompanied by a discussion on the rights and wrongs of conservation on the Somerset Levels. This emotive issue was still news. One local advocated the farmers' side: 'It's their land and they can't do what they want with it. They're not allowed to dress the land with fertiliser or weedkiller. They can only get a drop of hay off the land, and in poor summers not even that.'

The publican, exercising his diplomatic skills, could of course see both sides of the argument.

Parts of West Sedgemoor have not been ploughed for 700 years, for the thin crust of peat neither supports a horse and plough nor a tractor. Large areas flood, providing a rich habitat for wading birds and wildfowl, and flash floods in spring and early summer retain a suitable habitat for wetland plants. The resulting flowers and birds are a national heritage. The Nature Conservancy Council (NCC) and the Royal Society for the Protection of Birds (RSPB) certainly think so, and some of West Sedgemoor is now safely in the care of the RSPB. In the 1970s a drainage scheme was proposed for West Sedgemoor, but was rejected by the farmers themselves . . . many of the farmers were conservative and favoured winter floods, since they brought in much silt to fertilise their fields. After this drainage threat, the RSPB began buying land on West Sedgemoor, and leasing it back to the farmers, provided that it was farmed using traditional methods. A real political storm, however, developed with the Wildlife and Countryside Act of 1981, when the NCC designated all 2,500 acres on West Sedgemoor as a Site of Special Scientific Interest. The restrictions that this imposed on agricultural activities alienated the fiercely independent farmers of the Levels. Effigies of NCC officers were burned before the television cameras; farmers even borrowed an old tank which was driven ceremoniously onto the 'battleground'. Over the years, the NCC have managed to stabilise the situation, with more cash for management agreements, and more sympathetic public relations. Farming has also changed and surpluses abound. Once the foe, the NCC is now regarded as an ally, as a potential source of income. About twelve per cent of the Levels (around 16,000 acres) is now designated as Sites of Special Scientific Interest.

In these low-lying lands of Somerset, water from 800 square miles of uplands pours into a 200 square mile basin, and in winter the drainage network, despite extensive improvements, is unable to cope with the flood water. Huge tracts of this part of Somerset were subject to winter floods until the late Middle Ages after which the influence of the commoners declined, so enabling land drainage to take place on a large scale. The earliest villages were built on the highest land, as their names testify: Isle Abbots, Isle Brewers and Ilton. But disasters happen all too frequently. Sea floods in 1607 and 1981 wrecked the coastal defences of Somerset, and the locals still remember with awe the great flood of the Parrett in 1929. Somerset may even derive its name from these bygone floods, after the habit of *summer settling* on the lowlands.

My walk through West Sedgemoor was disappointingly dry. Few water birds were evident, though herons rose frequently from the ditches or *rhynes* and a herd of thirty-two mute swans watched me pass. A little owl bounded away, with its top heavy, undulating flight, between the stumps of *shrouded* (freshly cut) pollard willows. To the south-east, the prominent Currey Rivel ridge stole my attention, with its showpiece monument, a Doric stone column capped with a simple urn some 140 feet high, built by the famous landscape architect Capability Brown. It was commissioned by William Pitt the Elder, one-time owner of the country estate of Burton Pynsent, in memory of his benefactor Sir William Pynsent who left Pitt most of his property in 1765.

I photographed a small patch of willows growing on the moor. *Withies,* as they are known in the rustic, once covered huge stretches of the levels, and at one time there were over 100 acres on West Sedgemoor alone. Willows tolerate high water levels, hence their importance here, and depending on their use they were cut in a cycle of one, two, or three years. Willow is a pioneer species, and when cut back strongly or *coppiced*, it regrows vigorously. Green, one-year-old withies are used in basket making and other woven products. Two-year-old withies are more robust and tend to be used for the structures of baskets or hurdles. Three-year-old *poles* are less common, and are usually pollarded from mature willow trees for furniture

Withie shed, Stathe.

making. Beyond West Sedgemoor at Stathe, a small village on the bank of the Parrett, I actually found a withie shed. Stathe has been of acknowledged importance in the withie trade since 1810, and the village takes its name from the unloading facility on the Parrett that may have existed from the Middle Ages. Great billows of smoke along with a strange aroma had advertised the presence of this odd collection of huts. Its smell came from the steaming process, and was rather sweet and sickly. According to one of its workers, withie production is a struggling rural industry. Our conversation was accompanied by the hissing of steam. He told me about the process, when the stems cut in the previous autumn were rendered pliable for working. The numerous varieties of withies, with delightful names such as *Champion Rod*, *Black Mole* and *Black Spaniard* were dried, sorted and stacked for the basket makers. Different varieties are steamed in different ways to maintain the range of colours. My artisan friend complained that no-one wanted to work in the industry these days, as it was too much like hard work. His own son had tried cutting withies, but had given up the back breaking toil after only two days. A government training scheme had also foundered. He spoke of bad backs for the cutters and bad knees for the basket makers. To make matters worse, the bottom had

Withies and things.

dropped out of the withie industry because of the arrival of convenient plastics, and competition from cheaper cane imports from the Far East. It was a depressing conversation about an industry on the edge of extinction, with the hissing of the steam lending a nineteenth-century poignancy to the scene. Along the Tone nearby, a modern visitor centre restores a sense of balance and optimism to the industry, and I eased the air of melancholy with a brew of tea on the banks of the Parrett.

Burrow Mump is a prominent Somerset landmark on Parrett-

Burrow Mump.

side, and I thought it a miniature Glastonbury Tor. It also impressed King Alfred, he of the burnt cakes, who built a fort a mile or so to the west of his marshland headquarters of the Isle of Athelney. It was here that the Saxon, defeated and hunted by the Danes, retreated to the last safe haven of his kingdom, surrounded on all sides by swamps and marshes. The Mump's views over the moors were of great military significance to Alfred, as he bounced back from the verge of defeat to wage his successful campaigns against the Danes, to begin the unification of England. It is now crowned by a ruined church, which was destroyed during the Civil War, but rebuilt during the eighteenth century, only to fall derelict once more.

My intention was to make the village of Westonzoyland and the site of the battle of Sedgemoor before darkness fell, but I ran out of time and energy. I camped somewhere in a field on Weston level, barely out of earshot of some Westonzoyland teenagers.

# 3     The Pitchfork Rebellion

## Middlezoy to Weston-Super-Mare

I awoke to another keen frost, strong sun and an early start, with the promise of fine weather ahead. I had been on the road but five minutes when a bizarre sight appeared on the roadside verge. It was a long, thin, pied affair with legs, which did not appear to fit neatly into any genera of the animal kingdom. It transpired that the riddle was a stoat, dragging a rotting magpie along the road in its jaws, though I was only able to positively identify the beast when, sensing my presence, it dropped its prey and bolted into the long grass.

Sedgemoor was the site of the battle where the Protestant Pretender to the English throne, the Duke of Monmouth, met his come-uppance. A sign near the battlefield reads:

> Nearby James Duke of Monmouth whilst attempting to seize the Crown of England suffered final defeat at the hands of the Royal Armies of King James II on July 6th in the year of our Lord 1685.

The moor is no longer — it was enclosed by an Act of Parliament in 1795 so it was difficult to imagine the modern pasture and the dominant King's Sedgemoor drain as a battlefield. Precious little remains in the village as it was on the night of the seventeenth-century rout, with the notable exception of the church. The church records contain an account of the battle, and of the visit by the victorious King James to the village a month later. The mood of celebration didn't last long, however, for in the years immediately following the rising the infamous Judge Jeffreys, the Hanging Judge, toured the West Country, sentencing hundreds of rebel sympathisers to their deaths, and transporting many more. Protestant sympathisers were to be found in the West Country, and according to the historian Bryan Little, the Monmouth rebellion was an intensely Somerset affair; the county was his main recruiting field, his chief theatre of war and the scene of his final disaster. Twenty-two of the rebel soldiers were hanged in the village the day after the battle, after some 500 prisoners had spent a miserable night locked up in the church, some dying whilst the bells rang out the triumph of a royalist victory. Monmouth fled the battlefield only to be caught in Hampshire. His celebrated plea for mercy on bended knee before the King failed, and he was beheaded at the Tower several days later. What was remarkable about the Battle of Sedgemoor was that it took place at night on a large common

The Somerset
perpendicular,
Westonzoyland.

interspersed with rhynes. Neither side could accurately see each other, and the key factor in the proceedings was the rebels' inability to negotiate the terrain, and in particular the Bussex rhyne. Pitchforks and scythes could not withstand the muskets, cannon and cavalry of Feversham's redcoats once the sun was up, and the brave west country peasants were cut down in a rout, now dubbed the 'Pitchfork Rebellion' — the last battle on English soil. Conan Doyle's novel, *Micah Clarke*, gives a vivid account of the battle and Blackmore's hero of *Lorna Doone*, girt John Ridd, was caught up in the fray. Three hundred years later a re-enactment of the battle was performed on the site by members of the Sealed Knot Society, and there are some interesting photographs in the village pub of the 1985 clash.

Fifteen hundred rebels died during that night, and the memorial which was erected in 1928 commemorates them. Four satellite stones also honour those lost in the battles of Plassey, Quebec, Trafalgar, Waterloo and the Great War. I walked away with sombre thoughts.

I followed the King's Sedgemoor drain, which was tedious and sterile, a testament to the efficiency of the Wessex Water Authority. A yaffle on Pendon Hill amused me for an age, as I could hear but not see it! At Crandon Bridge I spotted a chiffchaff, the first summer migrant of the year which is always an excuse for a celebration. Puriton's village shop was neatly set opposite a vivid yellow arch of limestone, and a strange stone terraced cottage had a castelled tower set in its centre. As I admired this second wonderfully eccentric piece of architecture, a local resident told me its story: 'It was built by some crazy lawyer, around the time of the Great War. He done two of the things, one at either end of the village.' She shook her head. 'Then something went wrong . . . he lost his wife or his money or something, and he went and committed suicide.'

I crossed the M5 motorway, and saw to my disbelief a train crossing the next bridge northwards. No railway was marked on the map, but the initials on the side of the shunter gave the game away — R.O.F. — Royal Ordnance Factory. Lunch at a pub in Highbridge provided another example of Somerset friendliness — a resident of Weston-super-Mare offered me a bed overnight. I declined politely as a friend was coming to pick me up.

At Middle Burnham, beneath the ancient and prominent fortress of Brent Knoll, Meg's prowess as a sheepdog was put to the test. A farmer was attempting to divert a ewe and her two lambs through a gate, but the trio were proving decidedly unco-operative. Much to my surprise, Meg managed to turn the excited beasts onto the desired trajectory and through the gate. We parted amicably. The farmer had been helped, and I felt less guilty about being on his land, miles away from any public footpath. Scots, who are used to the wide open spaces of hill and

Tracks, tracks, tracks,
Weston-super-Mare.

muir, tend to take a liberal interpretation of where to walk!

Coastal scenery began to appear on the horizon with the cliffs of Brean Down, and the islands of Steep Holm and Flat Holm in the Bristol Channel. I watched four widgeon 'up-ending' in the River Axe. A flock of sparrows scattered in all directions and dived for cover as a male sparrowhawk dashed overhead. Wheatears on the saltmarsh beneath the crags at Uphill near Weston made me feel that summer was on the way; and climbers played in a suntrap on the crags as yachts patiently awaited the tide in the muddy Axe-mouth.

I knew enough about the seaside resort of Weston-super-Mare, with its piers, hotels and show-business bills to make a decision not to walk its promenade. Instead I awaited the arrival of a friend, Elaine, and we drove together along the seafront and along the toll-road to observe Wales across the Bristol Channel. Tomorrow I would resume my journey amidst the chimneystacks and smoke of Newport. In the meantime, it was an overnight stay in Bristol, with good food, hot water, and a bed.

# Part II    Wales and The Marches

# 4 The Monmouthshire and Brecon Canal

## St Bride's Wentlooge to Mamhilad

There are no better men than the best of the Welsh, and no worse men than the worst.

Giraldus Cambrensis, Welsh historian, twelfth-century

Into Wales, or *Cymru* as the Welsh prefer it. Wales is derived from a Saxon word, meaning foreigners; whereas the Celtic *Cymru* means 'fellow countrymen'. Wales is a nation with a capital city, its own language and a Celtic heritage. Yet it doesn't have its own government, merely a Welsh Office, and unlike Scotland it doesn't even have its own laws. Scots law has managed to survive the Act of Union of Parliaments in 1707, but the ancient laws of the Welsh Princedoms failed to survive the Act of Union imposed on Wales by Henry VIII in 1536. Wales is a sparsely populated country of 2.75 million, occupying 8,000 square miles. It is a nation of high land and rugged terrain; a nation of sheep. Perhaps because of its isolation and mountains, it has a fascinating history and I looked forward to a walk through Welsh time. I would follow Offa's Dyke, a border against the western Celtic tribes, the ancient earthwork built by a Saxon king in the Dark Ages which has largely survived to this day. Near my starting point at Newport I passed within a bowshot of the Roman military headquarters of Caerleon, once thought to be the site of King Arthur's round table. Though I didn't pass any of the mighty Norman castles (Edward I's ring of stone by which he tamed the Welsh Princedoms and killed the last genuine Prince of Wales, Llewellyn of Gruffydd), I walked through lands influenced by Wales' greatest hero, Owain Glyndwr.

St Bride's Wentlooge at eight in the morning was all a-drizzle. It was a cold, windy day, and Newport was a monochrome of greyness, the epitome of a dreich industrial landscape. England was barely visible across the Bristol Channel. On the east bank of the Usk, opposite, stood Newport power station, of Battersea design, with its accoutrements of pylons and power lines. Docks, factories and a transporter bridge completed a horizon that was a far cry from the pastoral lanes of Devon and Somerset. A grey container ship plied up the grey river towards the grey docks. Industrial camouflage, I thought, as I walked the elevated west bank of the Usk.

Saltmarsh and estuaries are marvellous habitats for birds, and

Shelducks flew low
over the dyke
    – *River Esk, Newport.*

as the shelducks flew low over the dyke, I could hear their soft whistles and gaggles of courtship. A heron passed overhead, and the crows were plentiful, ever opportunistic in the harsh conditions. I unwittingly disturbed a mother mallard from her nest, to reveal five eggs the exact colour of the dead grass with which she had lined her nest. Perfection. I hurried away, mindful of the crows. Redshanks were their usual noisy selves, squabbling in the fields on the landward side of the dyke, whilst skylarks waged a pitiful battle against the wind. An oddity was a raven, mobbed by peewits at the confluence of the Usk and Ebbw rivers. Ravens are very early nesters, and all mature birds should have been on their breeding crags by now.

Despite my antipathy to most things industrial, my route through Newport was interesting. I climbed the fort of Gaer for a view of the town which I would have missed on the riverside. The gasworks, transporter bridge and Llanwern steelworks would, of course, have been absent from the first Iron Age. Newport was the first Welsh town to ship coal out of the productive valleys. Its rare transporter bridge, built by the French engineer Arnodin in 1906, was constructed to cope with large ships and a high tidal difference. I remember climbing the thing as a teenager, dumbfounded that there could be two such bridges in the world, for I was familiar with a similar bridge over the Mersey in Warrington. It was possible to climb onto a high gantry, and watch the platform move its cargo across the Usk between its two towers. The town is also famous for the Battle of Newport in 1839, scene of an early Chartist uprising. One of the Chartist leaders, Henry Vincent, had been imprisoned, which

Transporter bridge,
Newport
   (*Photo:* Jack Sankey).

led several thousand Welsh miners and ironworkers out of the valleys and into Newport. Thirty soldiers managed to defend the town square from a hotel, and the battle was over in fifteen minutes, having claimed nine lives. The leaders of the revolt were sentenced to death, but reprieved and shipped to Australia.

Cherry trees in blossom almost broke out of the greyness as I hurried through the housing scheme of Glasllwch. I passed by a thriving horsy concern on my route to the towpath of the Monmouthshire and Brecon canal, which follows the same valley route as that chosen for the M4 motorway. The old canal engineers seldom got their lines wrong. I took advantage of a bridge under the motorway by a canal junction, to shelter from the drizzle and make a brew. A cuppa in these circumstances goes a long way to cheering the soul, and no long-distance hiker can afford to be without tea-making equipment! A flock of redpolls also played their part in restoring morale, especially a proud male, who shrugged the rain off his handsome red cap, neat black bib and cream shoulder patch. Towpath walking is certainly a recommended mode of travel giving superb views of the surrounding countryside, and because of the contoured style of canal construction gradients are never excessive. Alas, the Monmouthshire and Brecon canal itself is deceased, although a government employment squad worked bravely on its course between Malpas and Cwmbran, renovating locks and clearing out basins. Its shallow reed-infested waters were the haunt of moorhens galore. Most of the canal was devoid of water. Some parts had been filled in, and many stretches were litter-strewn and clogged with vegetation. One or two short lengths had been converted into amenity features, but its working life had certainly expired. One old lady, out walking the towpath, told me that she couldn't remember the canal being worked in her lifetime, but that she could remember the new town site of Cwmbran as green fields and hedges. 'Was it twenty years ago? Time passes so quickly . . .' she murmured in her soft Welsh lilt.

Cwmbran I found dismal, for it was raining, and it's a new town. Nearer Pontypool stood shiny new factories with their spruce chimneys; new industries of stainless steel, engineering and glass. I couldn't help but ponder that many of the traditional industries of South Wales were once so proud.

A fine piece of hypocrisy at one Cwmbran pub was more than compensated for by the cheerful hospitality at another less pretentious hostelry. The owner of the former declined access to Meg, stating that he served food on the premises, whilst his own overweight labrador blocked the main entrance with its bulk. Over a pint or two at my next call, where Meg was royally entertained with free crisps, the landlord told me a ridiculous tale of a coachload of wayward Glasgow Rangers football supporters who had come to stay in Cwmbran for the Wales versus England rugby match. If this takes some working out, the saga continued, for this match was actually at Twickenham. As a consequence of this inexplicable circumstance, the pub had arranged a rugby tour of Scotland in the following year, and had maintained contact ever since.

The canalside scenery improved immeasurably beyond Pontypool, as it skirts the Brecon Beacons National Park boundary. A British Waterways Board workman at an old toll-house by the canalside, built in 1812, knowledgeably recited the history of the canal to me. The Monmouthshire canal from

Newport to Pontypool was completed in 1796, to extract the iron-ore from Blaenavon. A tramway connected the mine on the hillside with the canal. In 1812 the Pontypool to Brecon stretch brought into being the Brecon and Abergavenny canal. Nowadays a mere thirty-three navigable miles remain, between Brecon and Pontypool.

At eight in the evening, somewhere on a navigable section near Mamhilad I tired, and simply pitched my tent. A twelve-hour day — not such a bad shift!

# Offa's Dyke

## Mamhilad to Pentwyn

The day began with relish, for a big dog fox trotted as bold as brass across the centre of the field opposite our camp. He left his telltale tracks through the frosted pasture, and the sheep in the field didn't turn a hair. It promised to be a fine day. High above the course of the Usk, the Monmouthshire and Brecon had been transformed into a rural canal that sparkled in the spring sunshine. Hazel catkins drifted in the gentle breeze, dog mercury lined the banks, and the birdsong was deafening. A beautiful comma butterfly attended the celandine flowers; chiffchaffs reiterated their arrival overhead; and an aggressive, territorial mute swan came swishing down the canal to treat us to several flypasts. Show off! Buzzards and a yaffle were other canalside gems. Mature alders, water-loving trees, now lined the banks. These are excellent trees for birdlife, full of food, and holes for nesting. Fresh clay on the banks verified the change in the fortunes of the canal with maintenance work ongoing along this stretch. I passed a quaint canalside scene of a cottage surrounded by ducks and tethered goats; washing hung on a line that occupied the towpath and a bright yellow maintenance craft was moored alongside. In the fields below the canal, small black

A big dog fox trotted as bold as brass across the field opposite our camp – *Mamhilad, Monmouthshire canal.*

Welsh mountain sheep and their lambs added to the rural cacophony. Springtime is certainly not silent.

Llanover Estate, lying between the canal and the Usk, beneath and to the east, has strange connections with Parliament. It was the family seat of Sir Benjamin Hall, First Commissioner of Works at the time that the huge bell was hung at Westminster. It weighs 13.5 tons and is 2.7 metres in diameter, and fully deserves its name of Big Ben. Sir Benjamin's wife, Lady Llanover, was known as the Bee of Gwent, and she turned the estate into a model Welsh village, transforming Abergavenny into a centre of Welsh culture. They now lie together in a mausoleum in Llanover churchyard.

Ahead the Sugar Loaf mountain lorded above Abergavenny. It has a peculiar shape, hence its name. Even more attractive to my climber's eye was the long whaleback of a hill across the Gavenny from the Sugar Loaf, Ysgyryd Fawr. Ysgyryd Fawr has long been considered a holy mountain, associated with St Michael. Persecuted catholics from Abergavenny held mass on the summit in the seventeenth century, free from the attentions of an avid persecutor and local MP, John Arnold. It is said that the huge cleft on the hill's summit was caused by a swish of the devil's tail, but the much less colourful geological explanation puts it down to an earthquake. Behind this lay the familiar hills of the Offa's Dyke traverse.

Trout fishermen were on the Usk at Abergavenny. I wandered across the flood meadows in between the dairy cattle, and into the castle and its museum, where I learnt of the history of the settlement that the Romans called Gobannium, 'the place of the ironsmith'. Gobannium was a Roman auxiliary fort, one of a chain designed to protect the borders of the province, and probably dated from around 60 AD. Wales was eventually conquered by Rome, but not until about 75-78 AD. The Romans withdrew from Gobannium in 383 AD. In common with much of Britain, little was recorded of the site during the Dark Ages, until the Norman, Hamelin de Ballon, built a motte and bailey on the site of the Roman fort, around 1090. A stone castle was constructed during the next two centuries, but the present keep, which is a fine-looking tower, is a trick affair, and was built by the Marquis of Abergavenny as late as 1819. Perhaps the most infamous prisoner ever to be guarded at Abergavenny was Rudolph Hess, who was imprisoned in a mental hospital near the town during the war.

I pottered around the small market town for an hour or two in and out of bookshops and topped up with victuals, then wandered out of the town via a council housing scheme. Unfortunately the minor road northwards was plagued by speed-merchants and a brew by the River Monnow restored an inner calm. A steep haul up a ridge led me onto the course of the Offa's Dyke long-distance footpath, an old favourite of mine. There was a reassurance and satisfaction about the campsite where I pitched the tent, for it was on ground that I had already travelled. A group of Scots pines near the tent reminded me of home. I was high on the Iron Age fort of Pentwyn and I watched a new moon rise above the lights of the cars on the main road to Hereford below. A little owl perched on the dry stone dyke nearby, an unmistakable silhouette in the gloom. Its presence provoked the thought that since these are introduced birds, at the time of the Silurian occupation of Pentwyn in the Celtic mists of time the tribesmen would never have had the pleasure of seeing a little owl . . .

# 6 Across the Wye into Kilvert Country

## Pentwyn to Bredwardine

Decision time first thing in the morning! I had to choose between a course along the route of the long-distance footpath and the Black mountain ridge; or maintain a truer line on three degrees and descend into the rolling countryside of the Olchon and Monnow valleys. This was difficult. The ridge walk I knew, and if dry would provide a superlative walk with commanding views. The lovely Llanthony priory is on the western flank of the ridge and is the very essence of Wales. Around 500 AD it was here that Saint David had his hermitage. He lived on wild leeks, hence the symbol of Wales, and died on March 1st. As a tribute, the church at Llanthony points to the spot on the Black mountain ridge where the sun rises on St David's day. But if wet, the Black mountain ridge can be a real bog-stomp. On the other hand, my real objective was to maintain this tireless meridian, with unknown territory ahead. So I chose the unknown route. I decided to explore the footpath at the eastern foot of the Black mountain ridge, and as I descended at an easy angle, the early morning sun burst through and created a fairytale backdrop for the woodsmoke from the cottages to drift across. The frost that lay in the patchwork of fields below melted into the new day and before long I was congratulating myself on my choice of track. The lower route was an old byway, full of mystery and overgrown brambles, interspersed with huge boulders from an outcrop above. I passed through a tunnel of hazel and hawthorn; bright, rusty bracken from the previous season coloured the hillside, and the rivers below glinted in the sunlight. Yellowhammers sang, ravens *kronked* overhead, and a woodpecker tapped on the ancient trees. I startled a rabbit, which ran at full speed into an equally startled Meg. An all-pervading noise of bleating lambs and sheep filled the air. Somehow the day felt timeless, and I shared the lands with the Celts and the Saxons.

Three small rivers drain this area to the south-east, with parallel courses and ridges of rolling land in between, until their confluence at Longtown. All of these I crossed, the Olchon, the Monnow and the Escley. They flow over bedding planes of sandstone, and through carpets of golden saxifrage. Another fine whaleback ridge, the Black Hill lay between the courses of the Olchon and Monnow. Readers who are curious about this

I startled a rabbit,
which ran at full speed
into an equally startled
Meg
*– Pentwyn to Brewardine.*

area, its peoples and its farming life, should read the splendid novel by Bruce Chatwin entitled *On the Black Hill*. This enthralling book relates the story of the Jones twins, who farmed along the Radnorshire–Herefordshire border (which was said to traverse their staircase!), and describes their attempts to come to terms with modern Britain.

I lunched at a seventeenth-century inn at Dorstone. Cromwell reputedly stayed there, but for good measure, the landlord explained with a glint in his eye: 'I've fixed a portrait of Charles I around the corner as well!' Near Dorstone Hill lies a neolithic chambered cairn called Arthur's Stone. Chambered cairns were communal tombs, probably used by a single tribe for several generations. They are among the oldest field monuments in the British Isles, this one having been built between 5,000-4,000 BC. Arthur's Stone was an introduction to the magnificent monuments from a similar era that I was to enjoy on Orkney. Opposite the stone, two farmers were busy unloading sheep from a trailer. I struck up a conversation with the leader of the pair who was a rotund, pleasant man with a ruddy face. In a superb border accent he told me that in his grandfather's day the stone had been much larger, and that fragments had been used in constructing the lane. He added that it was well protected now, however, for an enormous ash tree over the stone had fallen into his field rather than disturb the stone. Much to his amusement the stone brought many visitors. Our conversation progressed to sheep. I didn't recognise his cross-breeds, apart from the long black ears of the Suffolk progeny. Farmers love discussing their stock, and he told me proudly and

Kingfisher
*— River Wye, Bredwardine.*

with suitable embellishments that they were Welsh Mules crossed with a Suffolk tup. Welsh Mules or half-breeds, in turn, are the result of Beulah Speckled Face tupped by a Border Leicester. In character and friendliness, this Welsh border farmer could not have been more different than one of his neighbours, who was the only obnoxious farmer that I encountered on the whole trip. I was struggling to find the line of a footpath shown on the map between Arthur's Stone and Bredwardine, when I spotted him working by a hedgerow. Saved, thought I! Not so. In a most unpleasant and aggressive manner, he informed me that if I couldn't find the footpath with a map, then I'd better be keeping to the road. This taunt wounded my navigational prowess, and I retorted that it was impossible to adhere to routes that were obviously stile-less and which had been subject to agricultural improvement. A second farmer appeared from behind a trailer, at which point I decided to concede the argument. Although I am thick-skinned, and quite prepared to argue the toss with any landowner, I am also blessed with a degree of common sense. In this situation I decided that the odds were against me. I shrugged my shoulders and left. Fortunately, farmers of this ilk are rare, and the vast majority are decent country folk, who will bend over backwards to help a walker.

I camped in a wood by the Wye near Bredwardine. Late in the day it had clouded over, and there was no sun to highlight the kingfisher that I watched on the bank. A pair of woodpigeons copulated in the trees above the tent, surely one of the noisiest acts of creation that there is. I skinny-dipped in the river, a refreshing experience in the freezing cold water, though the towel suffered badly from the mud of the riverbank. It appeared as if rain was building up in the sky, accumulating in dark clouds

Bredwardine bridge, River Wye.

over the bridge across the Wye. In 1877 the Jenkinses and Merediths overlooked the bridge, keepers of the gatehouse and toll-collectors on the turnpike road. Turnpikes are the predecessors of our modern trunk road network, and the tolls and their collectors were despised by rural folk and travellers alike. Toll collectors have been likened by the historian Colyer to today's traffic wardens: '. . . they did an unpopular job in difficult conditions . . . subject to the vilification of some travellers and readily tempted by "backhanders" from others'. Dissatisfaction in the 1840s with the administration of the turnpikes and the frequent and varied tolls led to an uprising in Mid Wales, known as the Rebecca Riots. The rioters — whose leaders were always dressed in women's clothing — destroyed many turnpike tolls by night. The outcome of the riots was a government report which led to uniform tolls and toll-gates at least seven miles apart.

Other life in Bredwardine parish is expertly recorded by the diarist, the Reverend Francis Kilvert who was minister of the parish for two years, before his premature death aged 39 (a mere month after his marriage) in 1879. Kilvert tells of old country customs in the parish, such as a celebratory bonfire, *Burning the Bush*, on New Year's Day morning; and of great floods on the Wye, when cattle and railway bridges were swept downriver and many villagers' houses flooded. In those days salmon were common in the Wye, and were speared from the bridge at Bredwardine.

Safe from the salmon spears, toll collectors and floods, I fell asleep.

# 7　Marchmen

## Bredwardine to Furrow Hill

An early start in soft drizzle at seven-thirty, and by way of Letton, Kinnersley and Almeley to Kington. Waterloo farm beyond Letton, a handsome redbrick building, was aptly named, since I counted 110 dead toads in a 100-metre stretch of road. Much of the carnage involved mating pairs, not a pretty sight.

I chatted with an old boy at Almeley over a pint of milk and a rest, who showed amazement at my walk. A Marchman of fine stature, he was tall, with a weathered face and an aquiline nose which sported a splendid dew-drop. His attire was first-rate, and would have satisfied the byre or kirk!

*Old Shepherd*

Shepherd how I wish
I were as wise as you.
Old as the hill
With your twice grizzled dogs
that work still
Some sturdy sheep the Cluns.

I don't mind your dew-drop
Neither your dress
Ancient dark and dirty suit
Collar-less shirt or flat cap . . .
Nor grimy overcoat, Prince of Wales check
Your rope for a belt with Wellington boots,
Or even your red weathered neck.

Old shepherd how I wish
We could talk longer.

Old shepherd we could talk more
Of how the 'world's a goin too farst
Ar, binner-theys do this
An' dunner-theys do that'
Of shame-less politicians
'Ar, and that chap as goes boatin'.

Road sign, Almeley.

The landscape flattened considerably beyond the Wye. Mixed farmland dominated, with pasture, grain, sheep, chicken sheds, orchards and freshly planted root crops. I knew the country north of Kington with its ridges and hills to be difficult for a walker intent on following the course of *three degrees.* I lunched at Kington, a pleasant market town due east of Hergest ridge between the North and South Arrow, and barely two miles from the border. My acquaintance with the March farmer at Almeley proved to be a foretaste of border characters in the Castle Inn on this Saturday lunchtime. This was a hostelry that I had patronised on previous Offa's Dyke hauls. Nine locals sat around the tiny lounge bar. I was made welcome by these people, and enjoyed their conversation and banter. Mervyn Peake's *Gormenghast* came to mind repeatedly as I watched and listened to these rural folk play quoits, roll cigarettes and tease each other and myself! Meg settled under a bench. A portly Dickensian gentleman, with a ruddy complexion, smoked a pipe, and made most of the conversation and quips.

'You'm all dressed up today, Jack!' he addressed a colleague. Old Jack was a hunchback, clad in a shiny three-piece suit and a dirty tie. He had a deep booming voice and a tuft of white hair growing from his nose. Opposite Jack was a chap with a false arm, and next to me was an ancient who said not a word to anyone, and simply drank his beer, rolled his cigarettes, and occasionally muttered some advice regarding the quoits under his breath. Two members of the ladies' darts team and the barstaff made up the number. Conversation was earthy and rustic. Village bobbies and their merits with respect to licensing hours were discussed. One member had risen early at six-thirty to listen to the weather forecast, but went back to bed because it was so bad. Planners even came into the firing line. One of the number had submitted an application in the early sixties, which had been criticised by the planners for looking too old: 'This is the 1960s not the 1860s they'm said! Nowadays though, everything's got to look old ... they'm contradict themselves see?' He appealed to the assembly for support. Reluctantly I left this scene of border life, and resumed Offa's Dyke long-distance footpath.

The weather had cleared sufficiently to give a reasonable view back to Hergest ridge, site of the old Kington racecourse. Beneath the ridge to the south lay Hergest Court which in the fifteenth century was home to the powerful Welsh landowners, the Vaughans, and was for a time an important centre of Welsh culture and influence.

Pleasant walking followed over Bradnor Green and Rushock Hill, where I slumbered awhile. I admired the skill of a hedge-layer in the Hindwell valley. Hedge-laying is an old country craft that is kept alive by precious few practitioners nowadays, though conservation volunteer groups and agricultural training boards are doing much to preserve the old techniques. Today there are simply fewer hedges to lay, and the temptation for busy farmers to clout them with a hedge-trimmer is great. Machines are no respecters of hedgerow trees, however, and such has been the demise of the ash and the oak in the hedgerows that tree lovers must resort these days to tagging trees as a guard against over-zealous cutters. The skill of the traditional hedge-layer lies in selecting the correct limbs of the hedgerow bushes to part-cut and lay them at an angle, whilst weaving the remaining growth and pinning the finished product with hazel pegs. A well-laid hedge is not only a treasure to behold, but is neat and stockproof.

It is a remarkable fact that the Hindwell valley was a place well known to the much-travelled Wordsworths, providing a *three-degree* link with Hawkshead and Grasmere. Their family friend, Thomas Hutchinson, lived at Hindwell House, and around 1810 the poet enjoyed and was inspired by the ridges of Radnorshire. Rather less inspired were the comments in my notebook complaining of the ascent of Bradnor Hill, the ascent of Evenjobb Hill, and finally the ascent of Furrow Hill. In truth, though, this is an area that I am fond of, an area of ridges and mists, history and buzzards.

Our campsite on Furrow Hill was in the lee of some silver firs, easily recognised by their thick strands of foliage which are used by continental Europeans for Christmas decorations. They have enormous cones which make good trophies, but are rarely found on the ground ... usually they remain attached to the tree, and as the seeds disperse they leave the backbone of the cone as a distinctive spike. They were splendid trees, and provided a roost that evening for all manner of birds: fieldfares, jackdaws, magpies and woodpigeons. Imagine the noise that this lot made! Meg was in turmoil as I'd pitched the tent in the middle of a rabbit warren. Her sleep became one of dreams and whimpers.

# 8  A Shropshire Lad

## Furrow Hill to Bishop's Castle

Clunton and Clunbury,
Clungunford and Clun,
Are the quietest places
Under the sun.

A.E. Houseman, *A Shropshire Lad*

An overcast day throughout, walking the familiar territory of Offa's Dyke.

Offa was the Mercian King of the English who reigned between 757 and 796 AD. He had the earthwork built in the later years of his reign, principally, it seems, to control trade along the border. In the west lay the lands of the Celtic Britons of Cymru. Archaeologists have little doubt that a period of relative stability, provided by a powerful unified English Kingdom under Offa, must have existed for a dyke of such dramatic proportions to have been constructed. It was built along 150 miles of border, from the Severn in the south, almost to Prestatyn at the mouth of the Dee in the north. Purposeful east–west routes for trade were designed through the dyke at intervals. It averaged six feet in height, and sixty feet in breadth, a remarkable undertaking over difficult terrain. Previous earthworks in the area such as Wat's Dyke by Oswestry and Wrexham meant that the construction skills necessary for the task would have been available in the area. Many of the ancient Iron Age forts would also have used similar techniques. The earth bank is usually ditched on the Celtic (west) side, but sometimes on both, the variations suggesting different builders or parochial styles. That the dyke had some military function is manifested by the fact that its alignment is predominantly along west-facing slopes, thereby giving a superb watch across the borderlands.

The long-distance footpath does not follow exactly the course of the dyke; in any case, the earthwork is now only traceable for just over half of its original length. As long ago as 1955 the 168-mile route was first proposed by the National Parks Commission, the predecessor of the Countryside Commission. In 1971 it was eventually opened and became the fourth long-distance route. I had enjoyed the marriage of Offa's Dyke path and Offa's Dyke proper the previous day, above Kington on Rushock Hill, and was to follow this wedlock for around eighteen miles, finally parting company from both by the River Clun, in order to head east for Bishop's Castle. This happens to be my favourite stretch of the dyke, across the undulating ridges of Radnorshire.

A mile or so north of my campsite I passed Hawthorn Hill, which I decided should be renamed Scots Pine Hill, to pay tribute to the fine trees along its crest. Just over two miles to the west, in the valley of the Lugg, lies the site of the Battle of Pilleth, 1402, one of Owain Glyndwr's decisive victories against the English forces under Mortimer. His victory was aided by Mortimer's longbowmen, who changed sides. The scenes after the battle reflected the brutality and barbarism of the times. Welsh womenfolk shamefully cut off the Englishmen's organs, and dismembered and sold their bodies back to their relatives. Glyndwr, reluctantly at first, for he was middle-aged and had been schooled with the English court, led a Welsh rebellion which haunted the English for a decade around the turn of the fifteenth century. The pro-Welsh Richard II was forced to abdicate by his cousin, who became the staunchly anti-Welsh Henry IV. Glyndwr had by this time plunged into a legal dispute regarding his family seat in Clwyd, and was overruled by the partisan English court. Statutes passed in 1401 by the English Parliament would have made familiar reading to clansmen after the '45. No Welsh person was allowed to live in England, to marry the English, or to hold office. This was enough to fuel the

Islwyn Watkins antiques, Knighton.

wrath of Glyndwr, who waged a successful guerrilla campaign against the medieval might of the English army. Luck and the weather played no small part in Glyndwr's successes, and in one instance Henry amassed an army of 100,000 in South Wales determined to hunt out the rebellious Prince, only to return to England after two weeks of inclement weather in September! By 1404 the gaunt and ageing figure of Glyndwr, complete with forked beard and wart under his left eye, had managed to unify Wales. His triumphs were signified by his capture of Harlech Castle, one of Edward I's proud, and supposedly impregnable, fortresses. Glyndwr had destroyed the *ring of stone*, but he was unable to hold the unification of his country. Rivalry between the Princes was too great, and his rebellion faded into an enigmatic end. No one knows of Glyndwr's fate, and even today his nation is punctuated by a collection of reminders of his fugitive figure. A cave here, a hideout there. He is to Wales what Charles Edward Stewart is to Scotland, a national hero, whose finest hour was just by *three degrees.*

It was a pleasant undulating walk until a harsh descent into Knighton, through a mature woodland where Meg frantically resumed her quest of chasing squirrels. Knighton was founded by the Normans, and the town expanded after the influence of the Mortimer family, Glyndwr's great rivals. A Royal market charter was granted in 1230, and it developed into a major border trading town. Market days still dominate the weekly life of the town, and on Thursdays the town square beneath the clock tower is choked with people and produce. In 1854 the market place witnessed the last case in Radnorshire of wife-selling. Ruddy-faced Marchmen still grace the streets with a timeless air, unable to sell their wives.

The town on the River Teme has had a long association with Offa's Dyke. Indeed the long-distance route was officially opened here at Tref-y-Clawdd, the town on the dyke, by Lord Hunt of Everest, as a resident of nearby Llanfair Waterdine. The Offa's Dyke Association has its headquarters in the town, and a visitor centre interprets the history of the dyke to the walkers and tourists. Knighton has that small-world atmosphere of many border market towns. People greet each other in the street, and conversations in the pubs run around and around in circles as the friend of a friend of a friend inspires another twist to a tale.

The path up Panputon Hill north of Knighton sorts the men out from the boys, since it rises 200 metres in a mere half mile. It is steep and unremitting, but the rewards are the great views that continue with the walker along Cwm Sanaham Hill and Llanfair Hill further north. A fine railway viaduct spans the Teme by Knucklas far below. The Black Mountains are visible, some twenty miles to the south, and the view westward is

Up and over Meg,
Offa's dyke.

dominated by the nearby Beacon Hill. I stopped for lunch at the triangulation point near Llanfair Hill at exactly twelve noon, as a party of schoolgirls passed by on a sponsored walk. This was an appropriate resting place, for it is in fact the highest point reached by the dyke at almost 500 metres, and one of the best-preserved and most inspiring sections. I have walked this stretch many times and have often been humbled by its brooding skies and screaming winds. In fact in our family it is a traditional resting place, for one year my father and I set out to walk this stretch of the dyke, but ran headlong into a folk-dance festival in The Three Tuns in Bishop's Castle, a pub which brews its own beer! Our 'one pint' turned into 'two or three', and after a sing-

By the splendidly named River Unk, I admired a pair of willow tits.

song and several pints, we slept it off on the Celtic bank of the dyke!

Spoad Hill, immediately north of Llanfair Hill, is where the neolithic Clee-Clun ridgeway crosses the dyke. This was used by the Bronze Age peoples as a trade route, and many flints have been discovered along its course from Kerry Hill in Salop, to a crossing of the Severn near Bewdley. Drovers from Wales used the ridgeway many centuries later in order to avoid paying the tolls along the lowland turnpike of the Clun valley.

Before long I parted company with the dyke at the picturesque black and white timbered farmhouse of Bryndrinog on the River Clun. I discovered a lovely green lane from Bryndrinog to Mardu, with hedgerows of hawthorn and hazel and a mixed woodland above. In fact it was a delightful walk from the River Clun to Bishop's Castle, through the well-kept farmland and estates of south-west Salop. By the splendidly named River Unk, I admired a pair of willow tits, identified by their calls and pale wing patches. Three buzzards soared together over Woodbatch. Pale, pale, almost white dog violets adorned the hedgerow banks.

I had arranged to meet my father at Bishop's Castle. The town was named after its founder, the Bishop of Hereford, in the twelfth century, and arriving early I took some tea at Yarborough House. We met, and travelled to his home at Much Wenlock. After a shower and some traveller's tales, disaster struck: I had lost my notebook! Frantic telephone calls followed to the local police and the tea-house. Fortunately it had been handed in to the Wrights, proprietors of the tea-shop; and peace

Bryndrinog-on-Clun,
Offa's dyke.

descended once more on Much Wenlock. I believe that we retired to dad's favourite hostelry perched high on Wenlock Edge.

# 9 The Stiperstones

## Bishop's Castle to Westbury

It was with great relief that I was reunited with my notebook in Bishop's Castle at eight the following morning. I headed out of the town and across Lydham Heath where there is a heronry. The peculiar course of the Bishop's Castle railway, opened in 1865, ran across Lydham Heath. The trains reversed into the town after using a cul-de-sac siding here. According to the Shropshire historian Trinder, 'it was renowned neither for speed, efficiency nor punctuality'.

I watched an ariel battle between a raven and a female sparrowhawk
— *Stiperstones.*

Splendid estate parkland around the village of More by the River West Onny led me onto Linley Hill, from where it was possible to admire the afforested gorge cut by the West Onny. With a little height, the extensive walled garden of Linley Hall became visible. A magnificent mature beech avenue lined the track up Linley Hill. New planting had occurred in order to replace the ageing stock, and a plaque celebrated the Silver Jubilee Plantation of 1977. Treeplanting is a laudable activity, but I winced at the individual plaques that accompanied the many trees. Linley Hill gave wonderful views, particularly of the Stiperstones ahead, and the rounded cone of Cornden Hill to the west. A hare bolted ahead of us, and I placed my hand on its warm form. Meg also expressed a certain degree of interest. A yaffle called and the sun warmed our backs. A buzzard soared above Linley Big Wood, and I watched an aerial battle between a raven and a female sparrowhawk in which there was no victor. Female sparrowhawks are big birds, and a formidable adversary for most, but ravens are superb aeronauts, and this was a clash of avian aristocrats. Ravens, like herons, are early nesters, and it's possible that the sparrowhawk was straying over the corvid's territory. One theory is that ravens nest early so that their young hatch in the spring, along with a flush of carrion in the bleak hills. Ravens symbolise wild places, with their impressive flying skills and distinctive calls, *kronk!, kronk!* I have often witnessed ravens appearing and disappearing through the mountain mists, and have spent hours overlooking peregrine eyries, watching the falcons tussle with their neighbouring ravens.

Regarding wild places and inspiration, the Stiperstones remind me of that creature of pathos, Hazel Woodus, heroine of Mary Webb's novel *Gone to Earth*. This is one of Webb's acknowledged masterpieces, and is Shropshire-life epitomised:

> These thick woods, remote on their ridges, were to the watchful eye rich with a half-revealed secret, to the attentive ear full of urgent voices. The solving of all life's riddles might come to one here at any moment. In this hour or in the next, from a grey ash-bole or a blood-red pine-trunk, might come the naked spirit of life with a face fierce or lovely. Coiled in the twist of long honeysuckle ropes that fell from the dead yews; curled in last year's leaf; embattled in a mailed fir cone, or resting starrily in the green moss, it seemed that God slumbered.

A walk across the medieval moorland forest of the Stiperstones is a superb experience, with quartzite tors punctuating the long whaleback ridge, including the splendidly named Devil's Chair. Legend dictates that here the Devil presided over the meetings of the local witches. The area was declared a National Nature Reserve in 1982, nearly 500 million years after the formation of its rocks! A party of young schoolboys from Kent were busy learning to abseil down one of

The Stiperstones.

the tors, an exciting introduction to mountaineering.

This is an area rich in minerals, and lead mines have existed here for centuries, from the Roman era through the Middle Ages and up to the industrial nineteenth century. Five lead pigs were found around here bearing the inscription of the Emperor Hadrian! At their peak in the 1870s, ten mines produced ten per cent of the national output, around 7,000 tons of galena per annum. At Snailbeach on the north flank of the hill, and the site of one of the richest mines, a mineral railway linked the pithead with the Minsterley branch of the Great Western Railway. Snailbeach mine finally closed in 1911, ending the production of lead ore in Shropshire after some two millennia. Quarrying has not expired, however, and rock was being won from a quarry near Minsterley, which I passed later in the day.

I lunched by the triangulation point at Cranberry Rock, looking directly east to the Long Mynd, another treasured part of Shropshire. Since childhood I have loved the hollows, ancient trackways and pre-Cambrian rocks of the Mynd; its mists and heather, wild moorland birds and gliders. Only one glider had been aloft during lunch. Rattlinghope, the village in the heart of the Mynd, seemed a stone's throw away. Other Shropshire landmarks were more distant, such as Shrewsbury, the Ironbridge gorge (revealed by the cooling towers and chimney of its power station), and the Wrekin. The Wrekin is a significant Salopian feature, and was commonly considered to be the highest point in England until the seventeenth century! It was certainly the capital of Shropshire around the birth of Christ, governed by an Iron Age tribe whom the Romans called the *Cornovii*. Due north of my perch was the north Shropshire and Cheshire Plain. Sated with these views, I fell asleep in a suntrap in the crags.

Further along the Stiperstones ridge is an interesting area known as The Hollies. These scattered holly trees are probably the remnants of old wood pasture. Hollies were once pollarded (cut above grazing height) and allowed to regrow for successive crops of fodder. Believe it or not, young holly shoots are favoured by horses in particular, and a glance at the Ordnance Survey sheets for the area reveals many place names in the locality called The Hollies.

Snailbeach, now beneath us, epitomised the area. It is part lunarscape, with immense areas of white spoil, yet protected on all sides by Methodist chapels. Wales is barely six miles to the west, and the area was enveloped in the non-conformist explosion which swept the Welsh in the eighteenth and nineteenth centuries. Lordshill chapel, the nearest to my route, was first built by the lead miners of Snailbeach in 1833, and rebuilt forty years later.

Alongside Eastridge Wood, the chainsaws roared. Pontseford Hill and Earl's Hill, two more Iron Age hillfort sites, lay a couple of miles to the north-east. As a child I watched my father climb on the rock outcrops here, which doubtless inspired my mountaineering soul, yet strangely I have never returned to climb them. We used to walk the lovely wooded valley of Habberley brook, looking for pied flycatchers and dippers.

I walked past the quarry, which was all dust, noise and lorries, with the Iron Age fort of Callow Hill perched precariously nearby. All too quickly I lost height and entered the plains. I made the village of Westbury, and a rendezvous with my sister. A bath and a comfortable bed two evenings in a row!

# 10     The Shroppie

## Westbury to River Perry

The morning weather continued fine, and I headed slightly west to regain *three degrees*, as yesterday's enjoyment of the Stiperstones had drawn me eastward. Potato fields in the vicinity of Vennington were receiving seed of the Wilja variety. Marche Manor was receiving an external spring clean, a lick of paint. A pool near the Shrewsbury–Welshpool railway line held some wildfowl and our arrival evoked an exhibition of defence displays. Two Canada geese swam to the centre of the pool, calling noisily; a moorhen scuttled for cover whilst thirteen teal simply took off! A rabbit and a grey squirrel lived dangerously and hopped along the railway line.

I passed the site of a motte and bailey castle at Wollaston, in the lee of the much older fortresses of Middletown Hill and Breidden Hill. According to Trinder, more than 150 simple motte and bailey castles were built in Shropshire in the century or so after the Norman conquest, in response to the turbulent nature of the borderlands or Marches. The motte, or mound, was the central building of the tower, courtyard and stockade, which was probably of wooden construction, and the bailey was the protective moat around the outside. In fact a complex series

Canada Geese
    – *Shropshire*.

Rivers Severn and
Vyrnwy.

of Iron Age forts proliferates on these hills above the flood plain
of the Severn, and I crossed a small one on Bausley Hill.
Breidden Hill sports prominent appendages of modern times —
a monument named Rodney's Pillar on its summit and several
wireless transmission masts by the Severn. More modern
communications technology lay ahead, a radio telescope at
Kinnerley, which is associated with the Jodrell Bank radio
telescope in Cheshire. Huge quarry operations and scars at
Llanymynech, south of Oswestry, brought an earthy reality to
the sophistry of the masts and telescope.

I wandered in and out of Wales at Bausley Hill. Descending
this Iron Age domain, I crossed the Severn a stone's throw from
its confluence with the Afon Vyrnwy, and was decidedly
unimpressed. An uninspiring confluence, the rivers joined just
as two roads would join, with featureless banks, save three
sentinel Scots pines, and muddy swirling waters. The reflections
of the Friesians saved the day. Fishing notices were everywhere,
sand martins were not: it was too early in the year, even for the
earliest of summer arrivals.

Half a mile up the road was Melverley church, one of the
jewels of the trip: a small black and white timber and wattle

Three-sians, River
Severn, Melverley.

Saxon site hard on the banks of the Vyrnwy. Our old friend
Owain Glyndwr burned it down in 1402, whereupon it was
rebuilt over a period of four years. Its beams are of
solid oak, held together by wooden pegs, and its floors are far
from level. There is a Saxon font, and an Elizabethan (the
first!) carved pulpit. Adze marks are still visible in the beams,
and the date 1588 is carved in the porch. Altogether it is an
amazing building of breathtaking simplicity. Discovered in the
church records was the following piece of eighteenth-century
human interest (1776):

> This morning I have put a tie
> No man can put it faster
> 'Tween Matthew Dodd, the man of God
> And modest Nellie Foster.

At Kinnerley I took lunch at 'The Crosskeys'. Only two people
were in the bar, but that didn't adversely affect their wit. My
arrival (complete with rucksack and dog) was greeted with the
quip: 'What's the matter, mate, your wife kicked you out?'
Closely followed by: 'leave the dog at the far end of the room
where it's less crowded!'

After lunch the weather turned, and a rain came on. I passed

the radio telescope, through the village of Knockin (site of yet another motte and bailey), and entered a bridleway which led towards the Shropshire Union Canal. A little owl bounded away from my course on the bridleway.

*The Shroppie,* or more accurately the Montgomery section of the Shropshire Union Canal is tired and derelict near Maresbury marsh. Silt, reeds and rubbish have clogged its course. At one point Meg careered into this midden, in hot pursuit of a rat, and emerged in a most revolting state. Who would share a tent with such a creature? Fortunately the drizzle continued, and the worst of it was either washed or brushed off by the wet canalside vegetation. The Aston locks, beneath the estate land of Aston Hall, were disused and derelict. We crossed the busy A5 trunk road at Queens Head, now fast and modernised. This is a road I know well, since I've often travelled between Shropshire and the Snowdon mountains. It's a dangerous road, and Meg and I scuttled across. A couple of miles up the towpath, the water course disappeared altogether, leaving a carved trough in the landscape. Where the old canal crosses the River Perry, with a buzzard overhead, Meg and I called it a day and retired to the tent.

Melverley Church.

# 11 The Gresford Colliery Disaster

## River Perry to Rossett

An early start at seven-thirty, and we walked the black mosslands
through which the canal had been cut. Enormous teasel stalks
lined the canal. Soon I arrived at Frankton junction, where the
Montgomery section of the Shroppie turned south-west off the
Llangollen branch. An impressive flight of locks, the Welsh

Montgomery canal
sign, Welsh Frankton.

Frankton, takes the Montgomery into the Llangollen. By the canalside a sign read:

THE MONTGOMERY CANAL
Being restored by the volunteers of the INLAND WATERWAYS ASSOCIATION, the SHROPSHIRE UNION CANAL SOCIETY AND THE WATERWAY RECOVERY GROUP, for the MONTGOMERY RESTORATION TRUST with guidance from the BRITISH WATERWAYS BOARD.
Help yourself to more miles of canal by helping us to restore the Montgomery.

A fine challenge and a plea! The Welsh Frankton locks had been restored in 1987, 200 years or so after the canal's construction between 1776 and 1821; built to carry wool, limestone, fuel and grain. A mile or two up the canal, two old British Waterways Board workmen were busy cutting a hedge and burning the trimmings, so I gave them an excuse for a break and asked them about the progress of the restoration work.

'They'm been at the Welshpool Canal ever since I've been on the canal, ten years.' With a shake of his head he added, 'It'll never be reopened.' I asked how busy the Llangollen Canal was with traffic, with some interest since I'd barged along the canal

Chirk aqueduct and viaduct.

myself two or three years previously. 'Oh it'll be madness for the next six months — this week's seen the start of it. They'll be top-less, bottom-less and tit-less along here shortly!' After listening to complaints that modern holidaymakers showed no respect for their workboats, I bade them farewell. 'Ar, we'm got all day here!' was their parting comment.

Chirk aqueduct, across the River Ceiriog, is a fine construction, but overshadowed by the splendid artefact of the Pontcysyllte aqueduct another four miles up the canal, spanning the Dee. Chirk is interesting, however, since a railway viaduct runs parallel to the aqueduct, and it is a strange sensation to be crossing up high when a train rattles by. Here the two modes of transport truly run in competition. The railways, of course, were the principal cause of decline for the canals, and Chirk aqueduct provides a vivid demonstration of this. Immediately after one crosses the Ceiriog, there is a tunnel of about 600 metres to negotiate. I had taken the liberty of hopping onto a barge in order to cross the aqueduct in style, though I was unsure as to whether a towpath existed through the tunnel. One did, so I jumped off the barge again, electing to walk through the tunnel. Almost at once I regretted my decision, as the tunnel was full of diesel fumes, very unpleasant and revoltingly smelly. It was also

Roofs, by Ruabon.

dark, and I plied my way along with the assistance of the handrail. Meg sneezed her way through, being even more aware of the fumes than I.

A lovely wooded strip on both canal sides followed. Irritation and anger next, though, as I watched the moronic contents of a barge ahead spill onto the opposite bank and proceed to dig up the lovely clumps of primroses growing there. I seethed as I passed, feeling largely impotent against all this, knowing that primroses are disappearing rapidly from Britain, and were most unlikely to survive their transplant in any case. Selfish, selfish people I thought, but kept quiet, and spent the rest of the day deliberating with my conscience as to whether I should have rebuked the vandals or not. Indeed I should have done, since, frankly, they were breaking the Wildlife and Countryside Act by actually uprooting the plants. The incident dulled the day for the next few miles, particularly as I needed to travel alongside the busy Wrexham trunk road, the A483. Very seldom did I have to resort to walking alongside main roads, but I had to cross the Dee by the only available bridge. Hunger set in, so I patronised a fish and chip shop in Ruabon, and consumed my fare eagerly on a bench.

Refreshed, I nipped down a back lane, and resumed open countryside onto Wat's Dyke, viewing the Cheshire Plain to the east. Only the sandstone prominences of Peckforton and Beeston castles relieved this eastern flatness. Wat's Dyke is not nearly so prominent as Offa's Dyke; nor has it the luxury of a long-distance path, or stiles along its course. Despite the existence of a public footpath along this section, I frequently had difficulty in climbing barbed wire, thickets and fences, something which may have pleased the Mercian kings of the Dark Ages, who were noted boundary-makers. Wat's Dyke was built not by Wat, who was a legendary figure of Saxon folklore, but by Offa's predecessor, King Aethelbald. In this era, Mercia was in the ascendancy of the heptarchy of the seven Anglo-Saxon kingdoms of England. Northumbria and Wessex were strong neighbours to the north and south, and the Mercian kings were anxious to fix strong borders against Britons to the west. For the record, the other four kingdoms were East Anglia (which Offa would annexe in 793), Kent, Sussex and Essex. Wat's Dyke was a defensive frontier, possibly the first boundary which Mercia was able to establish, and designed to protect its Midland capital of Tamworth. Its builder, Aethelbald, was the self-styled ruler of the southern English, and held a powerful Mercia for thirty years until he was murdered by his own bodyguard. In the civil war which ensued, Offa gained power and continued dyke-building.

We soon reached the handsome estate of Erddig Country Park, on the outskirts of Wrexham, and passed the home of the

Gresford Colliery
memorial, Wrexham.

altruistic Yorke family who, since 1779, have invited people to
make full use of Erddig for walking, and to enjoy the
magnificent scenery. The Country Park is full of interest, and I
walked past the site of a hydraulic ram and another motte and
bailey castle. Erddig is now managed by the National Trust.

I was committed to walking through Wrexham and wasn't
inspired by a heavily industrialised town. It services the
surrounding mining villages, but the mines are here no longer.
Wrexham was therefore a trudge, and I hurried through the
thick air of a brewing town. My route took me past the Gresford
Colliery Social Club on the north of the town, where some
colliery winding gear had been erected to the victims of a
disaster. A plaque read: 'In memory of the 266 miners who lost
their lives in the Gresford Colliery disaster 22nd September
1934'.

This evocative sight changed my attitude to Wrexham. I was
raised on the Lancashire coalfield, in a community where mining
was important too. An empathy with similar communities never
leaves those of us who have been influenced by such an
environment. One grandfather was a colliery worker, and both
my grandmothers worked in the textile mills of Lancashire. My
other grandfather chose to leave the soil and spent his life in a
steel mill.

I followed a path northwards parallel to the railway line which
took me past a gypsy encampment. Somewhat gingerly I led Meg
past a massive pied lurcher, which defied his breed and simply
stood and stared at us. The woods by the railway line were full of
wood anemones, and were redolent of wild garlic. The track led

under the railway and into the valley of the Afon Alun, dramatic with tremendous back-lighting of towering and angry cumulus clouds above Bradley Fort. *Fly fishing only* notices decorated the banks of the Alun, the course of which was barely a few feet wide. I could think of more attractive fishing spots! I wandered over the dairy pasture of the Alun, over a footbridge, and into the village of Burton, by Rossett, where some friends, the Jenners lived. Lorna and Richard entertained the two weary travellers royally . . . I sank back on my pillow and looked ahead to the last day of this second section.

# 12    The Wirral

## Rossett to Eastham

North Clwyd and the Wirral were verdant. Lush pasture and great herds of black and white Friesian cattle speckled the countryside, brilliant in the spring sunshine. Milk production and modern grassland management systems had been finely tuned such that, incredibly, one cut of silage had already been taken by mid-April.

As I wandered through the Clwydian villages of Burton Green, Honkley and Kinnerton, the spires and towers to the east signified a fine city — *Deva* to the Romans, or Chester. Its medieval city walls and black and white period buildings make it much visited by tourists, especially Americans. ('It's Tuesday, it must be Chester . . .'). Beeston, Peckforton, Helsby and Frodsham Hills provided the natural prominences. Helsby and Frodsham Hills are sandstone escarpments above the River Mersey, which yield splendid views northwards across the Mersey Valley, over the south Lancashire industrial towns and coastlands, to the Pennine whaleback of Winter Hill above Bolton. Helsby is another climbers' hill, and as children my sister and I used to delight in the helter-skelter which sat proudly on its summit.

A disturbing incident occurred at Dob's Hill. As I was walking past a secluded sylvan property, a man walked out of the back door of the house with a shotgun. He crept around the side of the house, and released both barrels at something around the corner, and out of my view. I imagined that it was a squirrel. It transpired, though, when he held the grisly evidence up, that the object of his wrath was a poor starling, which was nesting in the eaves and creating too much noise for modern man. I stared at the starling in disbelief, and realised just how divorced we as a society have become from the natural world. The shooter had a hunter's smugness about him. I resumed my walk in a dejected frame of mind.

In many ways it was a great relief to leave the expanse of the plain, the farmland and the starling hunter, and enter the private estate woodland of Bilberry Wood, to the south of Hawarden. A notice proclaimed the woodlands as private, entry to permit holders only. This was good enough for my Scottish spirit, and I entered, declaring myself a permit holder for the day. It was a magnificent mixed woodland. Jays screamed, great spotted woodpeckers drummed, and coal tits repeated their monotonous shrill whistles. It seemed oddly out of place in the

Great spotted
woodpeckers
drummed
  *— Hawarden Estate.*

pasteurised, suburban landscape of this area. I watched a female
great spotted woodpecker feeding; they are easy to tell apart
from the males because they lack the crimson nape patch. A
chaffinch was bursting his heart out with song above the
woodland track. In a woodland glade which had recently been
felled, an estate worker was busy replanting. His attire was
superb — worn, torn and ragged clothes, and yet a tweed jacket
with a neat tie. Since I was only a 'permit holder' for the day, I
decided to take the initiative and engage him in conversation,
but he proved to be a typical old-school estate worker, and was
extremely aloof. Out of desperation I tried to goad him into
action, and asked him if it wasn't too late in the year to be

planting trees, but he simply responded with a shrug of his shoulders, and said that today was the last day of planting. Game, set and match.

Hawarden was a bustling small village, full of life which revolved around the row of village shops. I chatted to a local as I refreshed myself with a bite to eat. I had unearthed a 'victimised' ex-union man, from the Shotton steelworks, which I was to pass shortly. He confirmed that Hawarden estate and the woodlands belonged to the Gladstone family, William Ewart of prime minister fame. Not only that, but his diatribe continued into the politics of the nineteenth century: 'Not many people know that our so-called prime minister Gladstone made his fortune out of the slave trade and human misery in Liverpool'. Gladstone entered parliament as a Tory in 1832 and held office as premier in four ministries. He led the newly formed Liberal party to victory in 1868 over his lifelong rival Disraeli. My informant's tale of woe continued into the twentieth century. Shotton steelworks 'closed down' in 1981, although he told me that it was still 'ticking over' and employed a skeleton staff. Previously it had been the major employer in the area.

With relief, I descended towards the River Dee, away from Hawarden and my puppet politician. Somehow his conversation had been thoroughly depressing. Nor was it easy to shake off this gloomy atmosphere as I stared ahead at the doomed Shotton ironworks from the banks of the Dee, straight as an arrow here with levées on either bank. Three bridges spanned the Dee, a modern dual-carriageway road bridge, its predecessor the sky-blue old Queensferry bridge, and a railway-cum-pedestrian bridge, used by the steelworkers. I thought of my grandfather and crossed by the latter onto the Wirral peninsula. Wirral's derivation is from the Anglo-Saxon *Wir-heal*, or myrtle corner, an interesting reference to the habitats of centuries ago. For the present, the Shotton steel plant separated the saltmarsh of the Dee estuary from reclaimed pastures inland, which sported a new industrial estate for good measure. The enormous sheds of a modern pig unit at Puddington were surrounded by barbed wire and concrete. I wondered whether this was designed to keep the pigs in, or the humans out. Probably both. I was not having a good day, and the thought of animals kept under these conditions disturbed me greatly. A lane and a public footpath across several pasture fields led me to the busy dual carriageway of the A540. We scurried over, and came by back lanes past Oaks Farm and underneath the M53 motorway. Suburbia arrived in the form of Eastham. The American novelist Nathaniel Hawthorne warned against the 'cockney residences' which were threatening to engulf Eastham as long ago as 1854. Hawthorne was the American Consul in Liverpool at this time and knew the Wirral well.

Manchester Ship Canal
at Eastham
    (*Photo:* Jack Sankey).

Eastham Ferry, a mile down the road on the Mersey, derives
its name from the days of waterborne transport, when paddle
steamers left the Liverpool landing stage to ply the day trippers
of early this century across to the woods of the Richmond of the
Mersey, as Eastham was then called. Even before this, a steam
packet service linked Liverpool with Eastham, which was a busy
coach terminal for Chester, Holyhead and Shrewsbury. Changed
days now, for the Mersey shore is a continuous industrial sprawl
from the docks at Birkenhead to the refineries at Stanlow. Only
Eastham Country Park provides a hiccough of relief. Perhaps
the most famous aspect of Eastham are the locks which form the
entrance to the Manchester Ship Canal. The canal was the
source of much bitterness and rivalry between the great
Victorian cities of Liverpool and Manchester. In 1885, at the
third attempt, Manchester succeeded with the passage of a Bill
through Parliament, regarding the cutting of the canal, and the
Liverpool merchants' stranglehold on trade in the north-west of
England was lost.

The small square in the village centre with its war memorial
and red sandstone church with its rebuilt fourteenth-century
spire marked the terminus of my second stretch of the big walk.
I bought Lorna, my hostess, some flowers in the village shop,
and rested on a bench, awaiting the arrival of her husband
Richard. I was by the Mersey Estuary, about 262 miles from
Lyme Regis.

# Part III    The Lancashire Coast

# 13    Ainsdale Sands

## Liverpool to Southport

The drive to *three degrees* from my mother's home was deeply nostalgic. Speeding along the A580, the East Lancashire road, I was reminded of childhood visits to Liverpool. We called this road the new road, simply because the generation above us did, and we lived along a lane off the end of it. It meant the whine of engines and tyres to us, and the smell of exhaust fumes. Its verges and hedgerows were dirtied by traffic, dark ribbons of filth, which housed sparrows to match. To go near it and to be caught spelled certain punishment, so we left it alone. Nowadays it carries a small percentage of its former traffic, since it has been largely superseded by the M62. Our fortnightly journeys two decades ago were to Anfield, home of Liverpool FC, where my father took me to see Bill Shankly's emergent team. I stood on a stool on the terraces to enable me to see, and whirled an old-fashioned wooden rattle. I can still recite my boyhood heroes *verbatim*, and though I have lived in Scotland for many years, I still sneak a look at the English results to see how the 'pool have fared.

We headed through Walton towards Bootle and the docks, and to Crosby Marina, which was my starting point. The traditional infrastructure of docklands, the cranes and the towers, vied for the skyline with church spires and high-rise blocks. The first Liverpool dock opened in 1715 to export salt, and between 1753 and 1927 seven miles of dock frontage were developed. Modern signs still boast of enterprise, but the early morning quietness suggested otherwise. A cold, grey wind was blowing, sweeping sand across the paths around the marina, and heightening the graffiti on a wall:

*When the Wind blows the Cradle will rock*

Dog walkers acknowledged our presence in inimitable Scouse, lilting certain phrases almost as a Gael would. Meg and I hurried into the wind and watched the sparse wildlife of the marina, a great crested grebe and female red-breasted merganser. A concrete tower presided over the Mersey at the entrance to the docks, which seemed in every respect like an airport control tower. A lightship was tossed in the grey waves of the river, and I thought of Newport: grey rivers and grey towns in a grey Britain.

Crosby's promenade architecture was anything but grey, and

the villas of various ages and styles seemed to dance along the front, along with the litter and sand grains. My left hand performed a dual function of keeping my cap on, and the sand out of my eyes. It was barely possible to progress with any comfort, and poor Meg was troubled greatly. I frequently had to rub her eyes free of sand, as we struggled upwind. All the dog walkers seemed to be heading south and downwind, with dogs four times the size of Meg. I wondered if these monsters were status symbols or security snarlers. Plastic bags and polythene trapped on lamp posts rattled frantically in a vain effort to escape. Another symbol of greyness, a small tanker, plied its way downriver against the elements, swapping sand for spray. Behind the boat lay Birkenhead, the Wirral and a dim Welsh coast.

We passed a classic piece of inter-war architecture, a glass-fronted swimming pool, its heyday long since departed. The morning proceeded in earnest — a father and learner-driver son practised in a car park; and two old ladies exercised a poodle by standing thirty metres apart, calling the frenzied dog from one to the other. A modern coastguard station signified the end of the promenade and the beginning of a dune system. With this passing of the tarmac, my spirits lifted, and I was able to enjoy the fresh yellow buttons of coltsfoot. I was able to enjoy too the subservience of the small birds as they acknowledged the supremacy of the wind. Skylarks, meadow pipits and a wheatear sped by on the waves of the wind. Their calls epitomised this landscape, forgotten by farmers and even industrialists.

A yacht was moored in the channel of the Alt. So too were some pied sailors of the Alt, shelduck, so much smarter than the drab compound of the Blundellsands Sailing Club! On the beach behind the sailing club are the root stump remnants of a 300-year-old pine forest which once covered the area. Apparently the extensive sand dunes began to form in the sixteenth century, although their unstable nature has caused many problems over the centuries. Severe sandstorms in the seventeenth and eighteenth centuries culminated in the loss of many villagers' homes, and a church with its graveyard. Land erosion is a serious problem on this shifting coastline, and the removal of marram grass, known as *star grass* locally, was banned long ago. Marram grass helps to bind the sand, and is still planted today to help to keep the systems under control. The River Alt has changed course as recently as the 1930s, before suitable bank protection schemes were implemented. This area of Hightown was known as Fort Crosby during the war because of the minefields and defences that were laid down. Ahead of us was a modern defence establishment, and I wondered how the sailing club members negotiated the danger area of the rifle range which stretches over Formby Bank. The red flags were flying today, and, to be sure, boy soldiers of the Territorial Army stood on guard, and constant artillery fire cracked at a range too close for comfort. We wandered a myriad of tracks through shrubs of dwarf willow, resplendent with catkins. I skirted the MOD and ordered Meg to follow. She came to heel faster than any reservist.

A footpath took us alongside the Mersey-rail commuter line which runs north to Southport. The line was opened for nineteenth-century commuters in 1848, but for decades its cargo of asparagus was as important as its passenger traffic. Asparagus production in Britain long preceded the railways, and by the seventeenth century it was grown on a commercial scale. In the Formby area seed seems to have been introduced from France by the Formby family, well over a hundred years ago. From a peak between the wars of over 1,000 hectares, only about eight hectares remain in production to satisfy the local demand. Much of the suitable area was damaged by sand extraction, a more profitable enterprise than the highly capital-intensive and sometimes risky asparagus beds. If the asparagus beetle or rabbits don't get this unusual crop, then the frosts, droughts or sandblasts wreak havoc. Most growers had other incomes, to protect them from the vagaries of the climate. Cultivation of asparagus is a complicated business. John Allen, one of the three remaining growers, uses a bulldozer to skim the sods off the virgin sandy beds, and rebuilds them as protective banks around the plots. Deep sand is then used because it has few weeds, and is fertilised with dung to become *shoddy*. Plants then take four or five years to produce their first crop, and the costs of establishment are many thousands of pounds per hectare. If all goes well the fields are used for twenty years and then laid fallow for the next twenty years. British asparagus production now has its stronghold in East Anglia, so this railway line no longer carries spears to market.

Two trains clattered by, and a stoat cavorted along the path ahead. Ditches draining the farmland held more yellow spring beauties — celandine and marsh marigold. Soon we turned west, and took up the Lancashire coastline again, entering the second of a string of nature reserves. It is often held in the conservation movement that the public is confused by the plethora of conservation agencies, each with varying objectives. My journey up this coast revealed a bewildering tapestry of ownership and land-management bodies. I had already traversed a Borough Council Conservation scheme at Hightown. Next I came to a National Nature Reserve at Cabin Hill administered by the Nature Conservancy Council. Here I was 'pursued' by a thoroughly respectable chap in full country tweeds, complete with two disreputable bull terriers. I lost my path and found the high sand dunes hard going, so cut inland through Scots pines and the scented balsam poplars.

Somewhere around here I crossed Lifeboat Road, named after the site of Britain's first lifeboat station of Formby in 1776. The site has suffered the same fate as Raven Meols village in 1720, or Skara Brae on Orkney very much earlier, and has been buried, quite literally, by the shifting sands of time. Before its demolition in 1965 it continued to save the lives of many landlubbers, for it became a tea-room!

At Formby Point caravan site the mini aero-generators were proving their worth, spinning frantically in unison. After this came Raven Meols Local Nature Reserve, another scheme administered by the Borough Council, and home of the rare natterjack toad and sand lizard, red squirrels and the dune helleborine orchid. Yet I saw none of these rarities, and sympathised somewhat with a public accustomed to switching on the TV and seeing such wildlife in their living rooms. I knew that the toads are nocturnal; that the lizards are seen primarily basking on hot summer days; and that the dune helleborine orchid flowers in June! It is a difficult and delicate balance to create, between informing the public about why a reserve is critically important, and yet having to refer to wildlife which may be seen only infrequently, if at all. Conservation has to be credible, and few would argue with the reasons why these reserves are important. The sand dunes hold isolated remnants of reptile populations which may yet lose the struggle for survival. Because of habitat change and public pressure, the sand lizard population of Ainsdale has declined from an estimated 10,000 to a few hundred. Unfortunately, natterjack toads and lizards are not ospreys, and are not easily watched by hundreds of thousands of well-wishers. Perhaps, in this case, television is the key to helping these creatures. Somewhere along the line a group of British Trust for Conservation Volunteers were at work. I wished them well, on behalf of the creatures that they were helping to conserve.

The Scots pines had superb wind-trimmed profiles. There followed a wonderful mixed wood of sycamore coppice, birch, willow and pines. Magpies galore rattled in the trees and were blown all over the dunes. To add to the confusion, Formby Hills was owned by the National Trust and Ainsdale Sands was another National Nature Reserve, managed by the Nature Conservancy Council. At the latter site I found some strange flowers under the buckthorn, with distinctive leaves, which I later identified as spring beauty (*Claytonia perfoliata*). The buckthorn spines gnashed, grated and ground together in the wind like conspiring assassins awaiting their prey. I followed the *fishermen's path* towards the beach, where dune stabilisation work was being undertaken. In fact it was difficult to walk northwards, since most of the tracks traversed the area east–west towards the

A snipe was overhead, drumming
 – *Ribble Marshes.*

beach. We zig-zagged as best we could. Marram grass rippled and hissed in the breeze, not much friendlier a noise than the buckthorn. In one small pond, some toad spawn was strung out along the strands of vegetation. When at last we made the coast, it proved firm, fine walking if somewhat dull after the maze of dunes and woods. The sea seemed a million miles away, and only oystercatchers and redshanks relieved the tramp. My solitude was almost at an end, however, for ahead lay the Ainsdale and Southport beaches, full of the Sunday frolics of Liverpudlians. All was sudden activity. Nature Conservancy Council and Sefton Borough Council landrovers travelled southwards, whilst the shore patrol yo-yoed conspicuously in its lurid tangerine livery. Sunday on the sands. Cars sped by, as did youngsters on motorbikes, go-karts, racehorses, and huge Dobermans. Even Concorde flew overhead at a low altitude, on a trip over the Lancashire coast out from Speke, Liverpool airport. I was enjoying other people's leisure just as much as they were! Gradually the pier in the distance crept closer. Boy racers performed handbrake turns in the sand with their girls squealing with delight or fright. Big dogs (what else?) were being exercised behind cars, their tongues lolloping from side to side. Aeroplanes took off from red-flag runways on pleasure flights from the beach. A small tatty train on the pier, the 'English Rose', plied to and fro. I fell asleep watching the Southport Sailing Club race on the marine lake, with the pompous architecture of the seaside town as a backdrop. Southport is Lancashire's oldest seaside resort, and was successful even before the railways arrived when trippers were carried to within a few miles of the town by canal.

Kevin Peat, shrimp gatherer, Southport.

We walked away and out of Southport on the uninspiring marine drive. Large flocks of wading birds wheeled over the sea, so far out that a car would be needed to get there. A sand depot ahead had a somewhat precarious track leading far out over the sands. This area is part of the Southport Sanctuary, a national wildfowl refuge where some 30,000 pinkfooted geese roost on the intertidal zones of the Ribble, the largest concentration in north-west England. It is managed by the Nature Conservancy Council and the Southport and District Wildfowlers Association on behalf of the British Association for Shooting and Conservation. The final designated area of the day was the Ribble Marshes National Nature Reserve, which includes Crossens Marsh and Banks Sand. It had been an exhausting day for countryside designations.

I neared the shoulder of the Ribble and my journey's end for the day. Some shovellers were on the marsh opposite, and a snipe was overhead, drumming. I could see the fanned-out tail feathers which make the sound as the air rushes over them, but I couldn't hear it! The wind carried the snipe's courtship song far away from my ears, and I reluctantly awarded the day's honours to the north wind.

# 14     Good Old Blackpool

## Lytham-St Anne's to Fleetwood

Like Liverpool, Lytham holds childhood memories — of day trips to Blackpool, when the first to see the tower won a tanner, as did the first to spot the sea. Inevitably my sister and I shared the spoils. Lytham was always eagerly awaited because of its windmill, situated proudly on the seafront amidst manicured turf. Almost as imposing is the spectacular United Reformed Church of Lytham, with its distinctive white colour and spires. In the mid-nineteenth century Lytham was a larger resort than Blackpool, and earlier still, Southport across the Ribble was a thriving resort when Blackpool was no more than a collection of fishermen's cottages. Victorian Lytham was overtaken by the planned Edwardian town of St Anne's, complete with beach. Blackpool's beach is even finer, and has led to the town's eminence.

I began my day's walk at Fairhaven Lake, and nipped over the

Sanderling, dunlin and ringed plover – *Lytham sands.*

Good old Blackpool!

sea wall onto the foreshore. Southport was across the Ribble over miles and miles of mud and sand, prime feeding grounds for thousands of wading birds. Tiny specks of bait diggers toiled in the distance, like wading birds themselves. They were digging for the same quarry. Redshank, sanderling, ringed plover and the beautiful black-bellied dunlin fed near to me in the sand. Sanderlings sped to and fro like maniacal mice, and it was difficult to believe that they had a credible food-energy conversion ratio. The shelducks looked magnificent in the sun, unlike a toddler with a pail who took a nose dive into the mud, and cried all the way back to her mum, who guffawed with laughter. The toddler had become a dunlin.

I passed underneath a pier. Light aircraft droned incessantly overhead for I was passing Blackpool airport. The sand was perfect for walking, and as we neared Blackpool the sea became closer and louder. Yesterday had been dominated by the wind; today it was the turn of the sea. Everyone on the beach seemed to have a dog, if not two or three. I wondered how unsanitary and unsatisfactory this was, whilst trying not to feel too hypocritical. Blackpool's pleasure beach, or funfair, is dominated by a big dipper, much as in my childhood. What was

74

Blackpool souvenirs.

new to me was a huge man-made sand castle by the south pier, an architect's dream come true, which sat as bold as brass for all to question. Inside the sand castle, apparently, is a leisure centre. Beyond this pretender lay the real king of Blackpool, the tower.

In order to admire the tower, I climbed from the sands onto the promenade, only to receive a shock — the trams which trundled along their time-honoured rails were new! This progress came as a body blow; I had not been to Blackpool for fifteen years, and a modernisation programme for the tram fleet should have been predictable. I hopped back down to the sands. In between the tower and the north pier, two men were searching for rings and Victoriana with metal detectors. People have been dropping valuables on Blackpool beach ever since the resort became popular in the early nineteenth century, and modern technology can now find them. Metal detectors are unpopular with some, particularly archaeologists, who argue that the operators dig up vital evidence, sometimes plundering the finds and disturbing the vital aspects of the site. It always seems a sinister activity to me, sweeping such a device across one's path — yet some are successful enough to earn a living from their spoils.

Beyond the north pier, the sea walls became massive two-tiered affairs, to protect the prom from the winter gales. I tired of the beach and scaled these defences onto glaring white concrete, an inferno in the sun. I stripped off a layer or two, lay down on the wall and fell asleep. Later, the sea defences began to fascinate me. Concrete had mingled with a natural sandstone outcrop, and a workman teased concrete into flows. The resulting structure offended my eye somewhat. A kestrel hovered over the concrete. The need for the defences is real enough, for the Lancashire coastline is notoriously fickle, and has shifted sands regularly over the centuries. Two villages have already been lost, at Waddum Thorp (Lytham St Anne's) and Singleton Thorpe (Blackpool).

For old time's sake I hopped on a tram for two or three miles. In truth I was getting bored with all this promenade stuff, and yearned for the clatter, roll and trundle of a tram. As we trammed northwards, the grand hotels were replaced by smaller ones, and then by guest houses and finally by bed and breakfast places and holiday flats. The number of old people also increased dramatically away from the centre. This was reflected by the passengers on the tram, and their conversation:

Two female pensioners, of Lancashire stock.
'Ilda's goin' t'ospital termorrar.'
'O? What for?' replied her partner, indignant as
a wronged queen.
'Er uther 'ip replaysement ah s'pose.'
Well she wuz owt dansin last nite an' tonite, so it
can't be that bad con it?'

Our tram cut inland through Cleveleys town centre. Through the blocks it was possible to see the Pennine Hills of east Lancashire over the heavy industry of the Wyre peninsula. We dismounted. Meg had never been on a tram before, but accepted all in her usual stoical manner. She's been aboard a search and rescue Wessex helicopter as a younger dog in her SARDA (Search and Rescue Dog Association) training days, so she probably thought nothing of a mere tram. We sought the coast again as a bird seeks the air.

A groyne system ran northwards along the sands. Horses were being exercised over these in national-hunt style. From Heysham a large ferry headed out into the Irish Sea, bound for the Isle of Man. I looked ahead across Morecambe Bay to the Furness Hills through hazy cloud and saw the first sand martin of the summer. Walney Island and Vickers' yard at Barrow-in-Furness were also visible across the bay, but these landmarks were west of *three degrees* and not *en route*. I noticed a small pool on the map, and finding it over the sea wall on a golf course, was rewarded with the sighting of a dabchick. Such minor events fuel the soul of the long-distance walker!

We rounded the tip of the Wyre peninsula towards Fleetwood, the Lune and Morecambe Bay. Boats big and small occupied my thoughts, for a huge Pandoro Line ferry was anchored in the bay, and I stopped to watch three model yachts being raced on a marine lake. As I watched I listened to more intriguing pensioner-speak.

Fleetwood tram.

Two old ladies were sitting on a bench. At once one disappeared, with the sharpness of youth, into the undergrowth adjacent to the bench and emerged triumphantly with an orange.

'What is it?' asked her companion.

'It's an orange. Ah thowt it were an orange ball.'

'Are you goin' t'eight it?' The question was serious and urgent.

'O no!' came the shocked reply. 'It mite be injectted. It looks awrite but it mite be injectted. Yew can't be too careful these days. Ah'll throw it t'birds.'

'Birds doan't eight oranges.'

Her statement was ignored and silence resumed.

Beneath one of the groynes at Fleetwood lay one of the finest sandcastles ever created, with sand-pie towers and fluttering flags. Dad looked proud of his creation. I thought of Edward I and his *ring of stone* around the Welsh. It rivalled the impressive semi-circular North Euston hotel which commands the mouth of the Wyre. But Fleetwood's heyday is past. The town was a product of the railway from Preston in 1840. At one time it was the railhead for the London–Glasgow route, when rail passengers would transfer to steamers for arrival in Glasgow via the Clyde. Preston had emerged as the main port by 1900, whilst Fleetwood's fortunes were to lie with its fishing fleet.

We met my mother, as arranged, and sampled with relish the traditional dish of the Lancashire coast — fish and chips. To my everlasting relief, before us stood an old-fashioned Blackpool tram, at rest at its journey's end once more. Long may its bogies roll.

# 15　Medieval Monks

## Knott End-on-Sea to Lancaster

Knott End-on-Sea was sunny and breezy. Mother and I had a cup of tea in a too obviously pre-season cafe before Meg and I set off. Once again the tide was out, and over the sand banks I enjoyed the ripple of thousands of waders reflecting the sun upon their wings as they turned in unison. A dead sheep on the beach caused a detour:

### A Rotted Carcass

It is a jolt on the brevity of life. A rotted carcass of a beast — ewe or ram? Impossible to tell, there's a gape where the sex end should be. Or an arse-hole for the record books. It is an island of death in a sea of green saltmarsh, ringed by the trampled gore of the carrion feeders . . . the grass daren't grow here, not yet awhile.

It has died in the recovery position. The carrion feeders have twisted its legs and flipped over its hooves. The matted fleece flows over the ribs, and still covers most of the corpse. Beneath its ribs, an ideal cavern for some nocturnal shelter, the dung testifies its use. Bare haunches bleached by the sun. And the ugly grin of its ungulate head, eyeless, noseless and brainless. Its crown is bald, and its chin no longer. Vertebrae dance along its back.

There are flies, there is noise, there is smell. I am repulsed in the certain knowledge that, one day, I too will join the beast. It is a jolt on the brevity of life.

With this excuse I left the muddy foreshore and climbed a limestone breakwater, only to be confronted by caravan sites. The breakwater was a good place for small birds, and I watched wheatears, goldfinches and linnets, and the first swallow of the summer. Notices warned of the deep gullies and swift rising tides of the Lune estuary. Windmills on the map indicated problems with drainage — the North West Water Authority had constructed the breakwater to protect the low-lying mosslands of the Wyre. Meg was more interested in the rabbits that lived between the boulders.

Lancaster University campus held the eastern horizon, as I revelled in the springtime sounds of the sands and saltmarsh. Skylarks were singing constantly, and the peewits played and dived as only they know how. They are territorial birds who take no chances, and aggressively warden off any birds which stray over their territories. Redshanks were singing and displaying; shelducks crooned and somewhat comically appeared over-dressed on this occasion. Small changes mean much, and the informal path became asphalt; the limestone, grass; the sand, saltmarsh. Church spires and a windmill occupied my southern shoulder at Pilling. Apparently an old route used by the monks from Cockersand Abbey across Cockersham Sands to Pilling existed at one time. I marvelled at their confidence and knowledge of the tides.

On Pilling Marsh we passed a NO ACCESS sign (January 15th–Good Friday), designed to keep the general public safe from straying lead shot from wildfowlers. Sheep on the saltmarsh provided a bizarre foreground for the enormous Heysham nuclear power station across the estuary. I lunched by the Cocket cut which was a deep muddy incision in the saltmarsh, impossible to cross. Half a dozen teal flew off as I crossed the obstacle by the main road bridge. Not far away, by Patty's Farm, stood a notice which I thought was stating the obvious:

Welcome to the Black Knights Parachute Centre
No alcohol on the Drop Zone.

As I read the warning I noticed a small group of tree sparrows chirruping away. The roadside was littered with tide-borne debris, and the levée behind was a further reminder of the treacherous waters of the area. A knowledge of the calls of the wild birds of the estuaries is a useful asset, as first a heron gave away its location, *frank*! . . . then a greylag wheeled in, *kyow-yow-yow*.

*Greylag: The Scots Goose*

As a boy of fourteen, I was accustomed to the geese, wintering on the Lancashire mosslands; pinkfeet and greylag, with an occasional barnacle . . . wild skeins of geese that traversed the sky like the words on a page. One day, as a reward for some labour, I was taken by a 'goose-man' into the depths of some frost-bound bulrush, close to their roosting areas. Dusk was falling rapidly and our senses alerted to the noise of the reeds clanking in the wind. In the distance came the excited yelps of the geese, pinkfeet if tenor, greylag if bass. Suddenly the air burst into a symphony of sound; and dim shapes of blurring, pitching wings were braking but inches above our heads. My thumping heart provided the harmony. Thousands of geese fused into the blackness. In later years I have walked the reserve of Loch Druidibeg on South Uist, and admired the remote world of the nesting greylag. Out here, the dark peatscape of frenzied water is as black and desolate as hell. It is the home of the Scots goose.

Bank Houses hamlet held a converted chapel dated 1812, which set me humming the overture, whilst daffodils adorned the banks. Further on I negotiated more caravan-blight complete with amusements, youth club, launderette and shop. In another half mile I explored the ruin of the thirteenth-century Cockersand Abbey. The abbey is a small ruin of a chapter-house of a once larger building of Norman origin. It has had a

Greylag: The Scots
goose – *Pilling Marsh.*

precarious existence on the edge of the sea since its confirmation
by Pope Clement III in 1190. From this base its Canons became
very powerful landowners in Fylde, and would cross Pilling
Marsh with their ancient tracks and knowledge. Henry VIII
dissolved the abbey, known as St Mary-of-the-Marsh, thereby
depriving the locals of the light which they kept burning to
guide travellers across the Lune. The headland was an
unforgettable spot, with the abbey and a wartime look-out point,
and Plover Scar light on a bend of the Lune on a shingle bank.
As if by magic about fifty golden plover came into the field with
their haunting melodic whistles. A high spot. Fortunately, no
shooting is allowed on these sands, by virtue of the Wyre-Lune
Sanctuary Order 1963.

Up the old lane from Crook Farm to Glasson I spied my first
willow warbler of the year. Soon every inch of my route would
be resonant with their descending tinkles. The port of Glasson
came as a surprise to me, a backwater previously alive with
industry. Glasson dock was opened in 1757 and prospered once
the size of boats became too large to negotiate the Lune up to
Lancaster. Glasson basin was built between 1823 and 1825, and
fostered the trade links that had developed with the West Indies.
A year later, the Lancaster Canal's branch at Glasson dock was
opened, principally to carry coal, lime and foodstuffs. Occupying
twelve acres, and fourteen feet deep, the basin could
accommodate 200-ton oceangoing vessels, and carried up to
10,000 tons of timber per annum in its heyday. The basin
prospered until it suffered competition from the railway which
opened in 1883, and the larger and deeper docks at Preston

(1892) and Heysham (1904). It is still used by coasters and
pleasure craft, and looked resplendent in its pied livery and
sunshine. My diary also records Thurnham Terrace in Glasson
as being noteworthy, and an example of superb stonemasonry.
Glasson was a delight.

Ironically I followed the cause of the demise of the canal for a
further four and a half miles in the form of the Lune Estuary
coastal path, which utilises the track of the old LNWR Lancaster
to Glasson Dock Railway. Like the canal, the railway in
turn suffered economic decline, after a period of initial
prosperity when a station was opened at Conder Green (now a
picnic site!). The passenger service was withdrawn in 1930,
although a daily goods service clung on until 1947. Dr Beeching
finally swung his axe in 1964.

The coastal path provided good fast walking, and spring kept
up with my progress — willow warblers now sang in earnest; and
bluebells and yellow gorse flowers adorned the tracksides, along
with dog's mercury and crosswort. On a small pond at Ashton
Hall I added mute swan, coot and tufted duck to my bird list.
Only the shelducks, once again, managed to stop me in my
tracks, as I inwardly applauded their courtship flights, low over
the path. They came so close I could hear their soft whistles, low
grunts and the air riding over their wings, just as I had at
Newport by the Usk.

Huge pylons crossed the Lune, and as I neared Lancaster I
could see the castellations of the prison on the horizon.
Lancaster has had as many ups and downs as there are
castellations. Daniel Defoe, in the early eighteenth century,

Shop frontage,
Glasson.

described the city on one of his indefatigable journeys: '. . . the town lay on its own ruins . . . on a decayed castle and a more decayed port'. During the latter part of the eighteenth century Lancaster flourished with the West Indian trade, but became stranded as a port when the size of the vessels increased, despite its arteries of canals, west to Glasson and south to Preston. By now its strategic site and hinterland enabled industries based on cotton and furniture to flourish, and it has held its pride as the County town of Lancashire, even though Lancashire's administration was centred on the more successful port of Preston. I spent the last mile of the track in the company of an attractive local lady dog-walker, with a penchant for long-distance routes. She responded to my rucksack, stride and dog, and related tales of the Cumbrian and Pennine ways and the Pembrokeshire coastal path. She told me of Lancaster prison, of how it is a castle, a court and a prison in one, of its fourteen-feet-thick walls, and of its fame for trying witches and housing the Birmingham bombers. She also gave me accurate directions to my lodgings for the evening. It was a quick mile, and a pleasant way to finish the day.

# Part IV   The English Lakes

Lakeland Villages

## Cark to Hawkshead

We took a train from Lancaster, through the lovely wooded limestone countryside of Silverdale and Arnside, crossed the River Kent and resumed *three degrees* at the small village of Cark. On leaving the village we climbed an old lane up to Bankside. *Dogs on leads — lambs* signs confined Meg to her master's reach, since our route passed close by a farmyard. The farmers were busy fertilising their pastures. A magnificent cherry tree grew along this lane. It was in blossom, and had the flaked bark and the gnarled knots of maturity. Shortly afterwards we passed through a well-managed mixed wood, with a well-developed flora of wood sorrel and bluebells. The bluebells were in leaf with no flowers, the deciduous trees in bud with no leaves. A day or two more and the explosion would occur.

We crossed Cartmel racecourse and entered the historic village. The Priory was founded in 1190 by William Marshall, the Baron of Cartmel, who decreed that his parish should have an altar and a priest for the people. This gave it a function as a parish church, and thus his decision saved Cartmel Priory from dissolution by Henry VIII some 350 years later! Cockersand Abbey wasn't so fortunate. The Baron's twelfth-century decision saved some superlative features from the Tudor axe, such as a unique diagonal belfry tower, and the impressively carved

Steve and Meg on high
in Lakeland
(*Photo:* Bob Metcalfe).

Cartmel Priory,
Rowland Briggs's
bread cupboard.

misericords which depict contemporary scenes from medieval England. It's possible to while away some time admiring the array of pagan symbols, domestic and wild animals, and the ancient graffiti of these benches. Other attractive features of Cartmel include the pretty village square (complete with pump) and a fourteenth-century gatehouse owned by the National Trust. It has been used both as a jail and a schoolhouse! I admired the portals of some seventeenth-century houses, and resumed the racecourse on leaving the village.

Beautifully maintained hedgerows held masses of springtime blooms — celandine, dog's mercury, dandelion, primrose, wild strawberry and wood anemone. Bluebells and Lords and Ladies were almost there. I struck up a conversation for a mile or so with a birdwatcher from Manchester who was staying at a

Misericord, Cartmel
Priory
(Eric Hayward, 1989).

convalescent home in Grange. He knew his birds and I enjoyed his conversation. My route was beginning to acquire a Lakeland feel with the long ridges of Hampsfield Fell and Newton Fell to the east. I wandered some quite superb green lanes before the hamlet of Seatle. Something of a mystery developed along these lanes, as I passed not one, but two, three, four dead shrews along the way. I wondered why. Was it caused by a sudden cold snap, enthusiastic farm cats, or perhaps even a disease? Our next lane climbed a little, and gave good views of Lake Windermere ahead, and the high hills beyond. I continued to enjoy the hedgerow flowers, more wood anemones, lady's smocks and dog violets. Beautiful.

I lunched by the River Leven at Newby Bridge, beyond the imposing pied hostelry of the Swan Inn. It looked far too grand and prestigious for our ruffled state. Adjacent was the Lakeside and Haverthwaite Railway, a small private line manned by volunteers with three and a half miles of the old Furness railway branch from Ulverston to Lakeside (Windermere). It is steeply graded and uses hard-working little engines, one of which passed by as I reclined against a riverside tree. It was a maroon diesel and hooted as it passed. Its awful colour reminded me of Edinburgh buses. I crossed the railway and disturbed a pair of nesting nuthatches; their anxious whistles sent us scurrying away and up a steep climb out of the Leven Valley, away from the noise of the main road. On Great Hagg there lay the day's surprise — an active charcoal burner's site. Three modern (metal) charcoal clamps were set in a wooded glade amidst billowing smoke, old gypsy wagons, tarpaulins and wood piles. There was a real camp atmosphere about the place, and the smell was exquisite. Charcoal burning was once a traditional woodland activity, producing the fuel for Britain's early metal-working industries or munitions factories. A vast acreage of broad-leaved woodland was once coppiced in order to produce a continuous supply of wood, and burners simply made their camps in the woodland. Certain species of tree, such as hazel or birch, will regrow vigorously if cut correctly — at ground level and at an angle of forty-five degrees — and whole woodlands were divided and cut in cycles, usually 12 to 15 years. My wife, Kate, who has built traditional charcoal clamps in the New Forest, swears that they are an art form in themselves. First the cut wood is stacked carefully, leaving a central core to accommodate the hot coals. Small brushwood or bracken around a tripod is then used to cover the hole, in order to facilitate a final top dressing of earth over the entire structure. The final creation resembles a giant Christmas pudding! Hot coals are loaded into the central core immediately before the earth cover is completed. Careful tending of the burn is then required, perhaps between a week or ten days for a four-metre diameter, two-metre high clamp. Air holes need to be gingerly made at its base depending on wind speed and direction. Modern metal clamps have removed many of the pitfalls of the traditional clamps, but nowadays the supply of suitable raw materials — wood of the correct species and size — is not easy to come by, since most of our woodlands have reverted to *stored* or unused coppice. These copses of the Furness Hills were established by the medieval monks of Furness Abbey.

Unfortunately I was denied views southward over the Kent Estuary and Morecambe Bay by the thickly wooded slopes. Skinner Pastures, which is in fact a wood, had a roadside avenue of old gentlemen beech. I wondered if this was another example of a traditional woodland pasture, where livestock grazed beneath mature trees which were pollarded regularly to produce crops of wood for charcoal burners, firewood or dozens of other rustic uses. Unlike coppicing, pollarding means cutting the tree just above grazing height, which gives a classic lollipop shape to the trees. Like coppicing and charcoal burning, this form of woodland management has declined almost to the point of extinction.

As I walked these country lanes, small animals frequently rustled in the dead grass of the banks. At last I managed to locate a rustle, and witnessed the disappearance of the tail of a common lizard into a dyke. Meg can usually be relied upon to focus on small rodents in particular. Her ears, unlike mine, can pick up the high-pitched squeaks of these mammals. By Rusland Hall a peacock cried and jolted me out of my walker's trance. A buzzard soared over Rusland heights. A warm afternoon in spring, it was classic weather for surveying these raptors as they soared on territorial display flights. A sparrowhawk caused confusion among the small birds over Thwait House, until it too soared away on the thermals. Ascending Dale Park Beck was a beautiful walk. Grizedale Forest to the west held the lovely

A buzzard soared over
Rusland Heights.

young greens of the springtime birch and larch. The dale was
haunted by the calls of the ring doves and lesser black-backed
gulls, very different calls, but equally penetrating.

Higher up, it became a hard pull through a cold black forest
before the majestic view of Esthwaite Water and the Central Fells
rewarded my toils. Esthwaite Water was fringed with straw-
coloured *Phragmites* which lent a perfect contrast to the blues of
the lake, the sky and the mountains. I tried to content myself
with these thoughts as I flogged along the busy narrow road to
the west of Esthwaite into Hawkshead village. By now it was
trudging time, although I did take note of the splendid giant
chimney stacks of Esthwaite Hall.

Trouble at Hawkshead! One of my few bed and breakfast

halts of the entire trip and it took me three tries to gain acceptance for my wee dog. Twice poor Meg sat angelically, looking — sufficiently tired — at landladies with her doleful brown eyes, but even so was refused entry. We finally succeeded at the Ivy House Hotel, which was a delightful and friendly small hotel. Meg curled up in a corner and didn't emit a whimper all evening.

# 17      Helvellyn

## Hawkshead to Thirlspot

> I climbed the dark brow of the mighty Helvellyn,
> Lake and mountains beneath me dream'd misty and wide;
> All was still, save by fits, when the eagle was yelling,
> And starting around me the echoes replied.
>
> *Sir Walter Scott, Helvellyn*

The morning was memorable for its breakfast. I had been struggling from the effects of a gastric virus for the last two or three days, and had eaten very little, relying on glucose to see me through. At Hawkshead my appetite returned, and a flicker of strength began to revive my body. An appetite is a dreadful thing to take for granted, as is the availability of food. I was mindful of this as I surged through my mountain of cereals and cooked breakfast, to the amazement of my landlord and fellow guests.

Hawkshead has a similar cloistered feel to it as Cartmel. Although there is no priory to command the village square, the monks of Furness Abbey founded its thirteenth-century chapel. The medieval square and tortuous alleyways are frequented now by thousands of tourists in the season, lured by the picturesque, and the village's connections with Wordsworth. Wool traders and farmers frequented its inns in the old days. The poet was schooled at Hawkshead, in the old grammar school, now a museum, and lodged at Ann Tyson's cottage, now a tourist attraction. Wordsworth is big business, requiring a huge car park on the edge of the village, and a well-planned, traffic-free centre.

As arranged, I met some old university friends, Richard and Ann Greenwood and their young daughters. They had been good enough to leave behind the key for their home in Lancaster for my overnight, despite being away from home on holiday in the Lakes. We had agreed to climb Helvellyn together. We drove from Hawkshead through the winding Lakeland roads, bordered by stone dykes and history, past the Drunken Duck hostelry near Skelwith Ford, across the Brathay at Skelwith Bridge, and over Red Bank into Grasmere. This is an area I know well. I once lived in Kendal and was fortunate enough to explore Lakeland's nooks and crannies. Many a pint has been sunk with satisfaction at the Drunken Duck or The 'Brit' (Britannia) at Elterwater. Only fell-walkers and climbers will appreciate just how delicious the traditional beer is, when accompanied by aching muscles and damp clothes. Loughrigg

Croquet, Rydal.

Tarn and Loughrigg Fell once more appeared to epitomise Lakeland in miniature, and Grasmere, with Rydal Fell and Fairfield towering above, promised much to a hill man.

Grasmere is a pretty village which has also capitalised on Wordsworth and gingerbread. Wordsworth immortalised the Lakes, was born at Cockermouth in the north, and lived for much of his life at Dove Cottage in Grasmere, or at Rydal Mount. The Wordsworths were well-travelled folk, and William and his sister Dorothy visited many European countries, including Scotland, and befriended many contemporary artists such as Sir Walter Scott and Samuel Taylor Coleridge. He became the Poet Laureate in 1843, died seven years later, and is buried in Grasmere churchyard. His sister survived him by five years, and her journals are a vivid portrayal of life in Grasmere in the early nineteenth century. Of Wordsworth's poems, *Michael* is my favourite, and the powerful pathos of the poet's lines would move a buttress:

> . . . 'tis not forgotten yet
> The pity which was then in every heart
> For the old Man — and 'tis believed by all
> That many and many a day he thither went,
> And never lifted up a single stone.

A less eminent poet, Sidney Keyes, who was killed during the Second World War, has captured the quality of the poet and his beloved Lake District in his lines on Wordsworth:

No room for mourning: he's gone out
Into the noisy glen, or stands between the stones
Of the gaunt ridge, or you'll hear his shout
Rolling among the screes, he being a boy again.

The gingerbread came much later. It's made in a wee cottage redolent with the stuff, close to the church. It's delicious. You shouldn't miss the Grasmere gingerbread cottage. Simply follow your nose.

Richard, Meg and I took the old pack-horse road up Great Tongue towards Grisedale House, and began our ascent of Helvellyn. Richard is like a mountain goat in the hills, and I bleated my way behind him, complaining of my recent illness. I got no sympathy. Instead we talked of our acquaintances, jobs, and planning issues, and the mountain fell away before us. A wind was blowing hard, and the ravens were playing. I've spent hours watching these fascinating birds, since many of the peregrine eyries that I have wardened have had a rival raven's nest. Aerial battles are common between these avian acrobats, and seldom does a raven succumb to a peregrine's wrath. Ravens carve the air into spirals, fly upside down, and tease the peregrines to distraction. The falcons scythe the sky into slices and sit motionless on a rock throne surveying their domain, truly the king of birds. Ravens and peregrines are easy to recognise with practice by their silhouettes. A raven has a huge head and wedge-shaped tail. Peregrines are heavy-set falcons, larger than a kestrel, with a shorter tail.

Opposite us was Helm Crag, well known for the shape of its summit rocks which resemble the profiles of a lion and a lamb — best seen from the A66 by Grasmere. Today we were the lambs, and the wind the lion. We reached Grisedale Tarn, but barely stopped because of the pull of the wind, and continued onto and over Dollywagon Pike and Nethermost Pike. The infamous Striding Edge was ahead of us, dropping eastward from Helvellyn down into Patterdale. Of more interest to me was St Sunday Crag, across Grisedale, to the east of Dollywagon. We had been climbing on this crag a few months earlier. On that day a pack of Lakeland hounds was working the fellside opposite us, Eagle Crag. The baying hounds and the shouts of their foot followers somehow conveyed the spirit of Lakeland, tawny hounds rushing through the dead bracken and slippery rocks, searching for the rusty tod. Their followers were almost as invisible as the dogs, fleet of foot over their perilous way. As far as I could tell no foxes were flushed on that short winter afternoon.

Helvellyn's summit was surprisingly busy for the early season and wind. It is possibly the most climbed Lakeland hill, being much more accessible than Scafell Pike, England's highest mountain over to the west. Helvellyn's first recorded climber was

Captain Joseph Budworth who recorded the ascent in his book of 1792, *A Fortnight's Ramble in the Lakes*. He amused himself by rolling boulders down the mountainside, a tactic which flaunts current mountain safety codes. Famous people have toiled to its summit, and on one historic occasion, Wordsworth, Scott and Sir Humphry Davy (of Davy lamp fame) were gathered together. Helvellyn is famous for the story of Gough and his dog, as romanticised by Scott. Gough was a young man killed 'in the arms of Helvellyn and Catchedicam' whose corpse was discovered months after with his dog still guarding his body: '. . . the much-loved remains of her master defended, and chased the hill-fox and the raven away'. Old snow cornices clung to the eastern edge in a vain attempt to hold back the year. It had been a long time since I had seen so many people (around a dozen or so) on a summit, probably because I avoid popular hills in mid-season. A slate memorial on the summit reads:

> The first aeroplane to land on a mountain in Great Britain did so on this spot on December 22nd 1926. John Leeming and Bert Hinckler in an Avro 583 Gosport landed here and after a short stay flew back to Woodford.

After our short stay we headed north-west off the hill, down White Side towards the Thirlspot Inn. I couldn't help but reflect that Thirlmere is such an obvious man-made feature, with its draw-down scars and circumference of conifers. As we lolloped downwards, someone suggested a pint. Meg got the blame. We searched our pockets for coins and scraped together enough for a couple. It was all academic: the pub had closed by the time we reached it. Thirlmere's revenge.

# Blencathra to Eden

## Scales to Carlisle

The White Horse Inn at Scales is a favourite starting place for playing on Blencathra, the hill which towers above the A66 Penrith to Keswick road. Blencathra is a much more interesting hill than its western neighbour, Skiddaw, because of the series of ridges which spread southward from its summit. They are not hard climbing ridges, but offer delightful scrambles, and Kate and I have often enjoyed Sharp Edge and Hall's Fell ridge.

Today, though, it was drizzling, and Blencathra was lost in a sea of mist. My trusty climbing pal Bob Metcalfe dropped me off and grinned at the Lakeland drizzle. 'See you in a few weeks, youth!' he said and drove off back to Whitehaven, his car enveloped, as usual, in a cloud of pipe-tobacco smoke. I had stayed overnight with Bob, Chris and the kids at Lowca by Whitehaven. Optimistically I'd hoped for a pint or two of Jennings, but tiredness set in and the household had turned in early. It has long been held that the finest things to emerge from Cockermouth are William Wordsworth and Jennings's Best Bitter. I'm not sure about the order of preference.

I peered into the mist and set off. Willow warblers were competing well with the noise of traffic, but the overriding sensation was the smell of the hill, rank with the mix of lanolin and sheep dung. A roadside ditch held tadpoles. By Southerfell

Keswick & Latrigg Fell.

Barn door, Souther Fell.

farmhouse I walked past a domestic dispute. Just as I was admiring its barn door dated 1699; a man emerged from another doorway and spoke back to it — 'Stop being so childish, you're not a little baby!' His spleen vent, he departed, leaving the baby at home. I hurried away.

Our track beneath the weight of Blencathra's Souther Fell was of the hills, of drizzle and sheep, of wet rocks and black crows. Mungrisdale hamlet was truly rural, with smithy cottages, the Mill Inn and a mother pushing her baby in a pram. A rookery added to its noise. The burn which flows through the village revels in the fine name of the River Glenderamackin, and revealed secrets in the gloom of the rugged Bannerdale crags. Over to the east the landscape became the tamer forests and pastures of Greystoke Park. Beyond Mungrisdale the jackdaws had conquered Raven Crag, and an argumentative lot they were too.

A fine old packhorse bridge crosses the Caldew at Mosedale, another mile to the north, where I rested and drummed up. Ancient history lorded over us in the form of Carrock Fell and its Iron-Age fort. An old house dated 1722 had some initials over the doorway, which is a habit common in Lakeland, those of the mason or the original married couple. This concern had a fine steading, and a beautiful herd of brown and white Ayrshire cattle tended by herdsmen and women kitted out with smart blue Ford overalls.

A heron flapped away, over the Caldew. From some boulders high on Carrock Fell a ring ouzel sang its simple plaintive song. It was a timeless sound, and I imagined that 2,000 years ago its song may have been recognised as a harbinger of summer by the community living on the hilltop. I crossed a ford over Carrock Beck and noticed a swarm of kids in orange waterproofs on the hillside. Their source was a yellow Cumbria County Council minibus parked by the trackside. 'Orienteering — or trying', volunteered their instructor, munching a sandwich. I tried to interpret the emphasis he placed on the 'trying'. Somehow instructors have a resigned look about them, born of repetition. Skylarks sang their hearts out above Caldbeck Common. I was almost 1,000 feet high by now at Calebrack, and through the murk ahead could just make out Carlisle, the border city. Another prominence on the horizon was a modern aero-generator near Newlands. I awarded myself a gold star for observation for spotting some moschatel 'town hall clocks' in the hedgerow. These unusual early flowers are by no means easy to see, but once seen are never to be forgotten because of their distinctive appearance. If you're blessed with a good imagination, their flower head resembles a clock face.

The twin blades of the aero-generator turned slowly capturing a force which man has harnessed over the centuries. The cost of this plant was visual, and my thoughts turned to power generation. The problem of course is not really how to generate the power, but at what cost, both economic and environmental. The penalties of power production, nuclear, fossil fuel, wind and water, stayed with me for a mile or so (and would return in Orkney), until I was presented with a practical problem of my own. I had followed a track down to the Caldew, and hoped to assume a bridleway on the opposite bank. Unfortunately I failed to notice the lack of a bridge, and stared at the rushing water. A grey wagtail, smart as a tailor's dummy, visited rock after rock midstream. 'Come on over', he seemed to say. Meg was keen, but she likes water. There was no alternative, and so I removed my boots, swung them behind my neck and waded over as carefully as the icy water and slippery rocks would permit. That water was cold! I celebrated on the opposite bank with lunch, and sat with the scent of crushed garlic leaves, and the gurgle of the river.

The bridleway along the Caldew was heavy going, since it was poorly drained and well used. Its course was magnificent, through a verdant ash and hazel woodland dressed in green mosses and ferns, and all the typical woodland flowers of the season. Water raced through the bedding planes in the river below and tugged at the colonies of woodrush and golden saxifrage. The woodland left the river, and became managed

A grey wagtail, smart
as a tailor's dummy,
visited rock after rock
midstream
   — *River Caldew.*

and keepered. Disappointment. I played cat and mouse with the
Caldew for several more miles, sometimes walking on the
riverside, and at other times not. I enjoyed the Caldew — it was
racy and tumbled over horizontal strata; it seemed as anxious as
I was to reach Carlisle. An old sluice system and lade for a
riverside mill was crossed, near a small flock of common gulls.
Next came an equestrian course in a field, then we were howled
at on the opposite bank by a basset hound. 'Ugly, bad tempered
old thing,' thought Meg.

Near the prestigious Rose Castle I struck up a conversation
with a fly-fisherman who had called it a day. Without luck, he
spoke enthusiastically of the big brown trout in the river, 'three
to four pounders', and how hopeful he was that in a year or
two's time the salmon would return now that some fish ladders
had been constructed downstream. Lime House, a large private
school, was amok with blue mini-buses and schoolchildren. Our
arrival coincided with their departure. We pressed on through
the light industry of the converted mills of Bridgend and
Buckabank, and into the village of Dalston. Dalston and
Cummersdale, satellites of Carlisle, were surprisingly industrial,
with large plants operated by Nestlé and Pirelli respectively. I
caught a bus for the last three miles into the city in order to
avoid the tramp through the suburbs.

Carlisle is known as the border city and has suffered centuries
of turbulence because of its location. The Roman general
Agricola is usually acknowledged as its founder in 80AD. There
is little evidence of a pre-Roman settlement, though it quickly
became a significant Roman fort of over 1,000 soldiers,
responsible for surveillance of the western reaches of Hadrian's

Wall. Romans occupied its city walls for a little over 300 years. Its Roman name of *Luguvalium* became corrupted to *luel* and prefixed by the British word for fort, *caer*, hence Carlisle. During the Dark Ages the once prosperous city was sacked by the Danes and ruined. At the time of the Norman conquest it was considered to be Scottish territory and has the distinction of being the only city to be added to England since the Domesday Book. It was William II (*Rufus*) who restored the city, built a castle, and gave Carlisle her Englishness, despite the tugs of war which ensued over the medieval era. To the north the area became known as the Debatable Land, a hostile place even in times of peace; beyond the walls lay mosses and marshlands, the haunt of moss-troopers and thieves, and home to the wild clans of Armstrong and Graham. Plagues and fires bedevilled the city, and sieges lapped its walls. In the mid-sixteenth century it was decreed that no Scotsman might walk in the city after a curfew bell had been sounded in the evening. During the Civil War in 1645 Royalist Carlisle endured an eight-month siege which was lost with honour to the Scots general Lesley. By the Act of Union in 1707 Scotsmen could enter the city on payment of the usual single toll rather than the double penalty levied prior to Union. Bonnie Prince Charlie virtually walked through the walls, for its citizens were weary of strife, the castle's defences in disrepair, and its troubled times were almost at an end. Butcher Cumberland even called Carlisle Castle 'the old hen coop', and routed the Jacobite presence in a mere two days, thus ending the last siege of any English city. After the '45 the textile trade flourished along the Caldew which led to further development such as brewing and service industries. In 1847 the railway era began, and the border city at last became a peaceful centre for the Debatable Land of the Marches.

I stood on the bridge over the Eden, and saw from its plaque that it had been erected at the time of Waterloo, 1815. I overlooked Carlisle Cricket Club where my route headed west, then north along the Eden, but first I had an overnight stay and a welcome from Norman and Elsie, folk as Cumbrian as the Eden, and kind, hospitable folk at that.

# 19     The Border City

## Carlisle to Gretna

I made a poor decision, and paid for it with a tough start along the Eden. Paradise it certainly wasn't, and I battled my way along a fishermen's track of sorts, fighting across fallen trees, up embankments and down, through mud and undergrowth. In no time at all I was hot and bothered, and in an unsympathetic mood for a day's hike. I persevered, having once attempted to abandon the riverside by climbing the bank only to find myself by a fence bordering a well-heeled residence. Reluctantly I resumed the fray, and eventually emerged below the youth hostel and onto open pasture. Relief. Across the river an old power station was being demolished. Norman had told me that this was a popular spot for boys to swim, since the water was warm here. Just along from the power station was the disused Caledonian railway bridge which Norman had earmarked for a bypass scheme for the city, but doubting whether the planners had as much vision as he.

This was a landscape of pylons and pasture, of levées, a lazy river and its wildlife. A heron fished on the bank opposite and half a dozen male mallards, their seasonal tasks complete, preened with self-importance. The females would be part of the undergrowth somewhere. Two cormorants flew downstream,

Sand martins flashed along the river and its sandbanks
— *River Eden.*

then two greylags full of bluster flew upstream. A large fish jumped. Magpies were everywhere. Meg chased rabbits, and I enjoyed my solitude with the wildlife. Grinsdale church tower, prominent on a bend in the river on the opposite bank, was mostly hidden by a copse of trees and a ruined wall.

Migrants were appearing more frequently now, and sand martins flashed along the river and its sandbanks. I wished them well for they had recently experienced ill fortune and a population crash caused by extreme temperatures on migration in Africa. Common sandpipers trilled their songs along the water's edge, bobbing their tails and flickering their wings across the water. With the help of these creatures I recovered my humour. A sandstone bluff gave us a precarious path above the deep swirling muddy waters; orange liverworts were encrusted on its oozing walls. I spent an age watching some goosanders displaying on the river. A male courted two females, and would toss his bottle-green head spectacularly in the air. At first the two females preened nonchalantly and appeared completely uninterested in his antics. When he began to move away, however, one of the females followed — so progress was being made after all. The females have neck markings with an abrupt colour change from a brown head to a white neck, which is the surest way of differentiating them from the similar female red-breasted mergansers.

We passed through a riverside menagerie of chickens, cockerels, geese and ducks. For variety I took a track parallel with the river for a short time but found it waterlogged and hard going. Field edges took over from a track on the riverside which also made hard, tacky going. I yearned for a change, and felt relieved when the river swung northwards to the village of Rockcliffe. Next the river swings west and together with the Esk forms an area of saltmarsh, the haunt of wind and wildfowl. As I admired an old railway hut relocated and transformed into a riverside howf (rough shelter), I heard the distinctive trumpeting of a whooper swan. It was in the company of three mute swans, which was unusual. I was reminded of home, for in the early part of winter some 200 of these beautiful creatures from Iceland stay on Loch Leven. One unforgettable early morning, Kate, my father and I were on a hillside above the loch standing in mist listening to the haunting calls of these ghosts from the north. Their calls became stronger, until, in a train of timelessness, their shapes came melting through the mists and over our heads. Such moments of poetry of form and elegance are rare in a lifetime, and that dawn we were spellbound by the whoopers' power. There is a folksong which tells of a hunter who mistakenly shoots his lover as he takes her for a swan. Swans are like that.

The spire of Rockcliffe-with-Cargo parish church performed

well as a local landmark. As we passed, the porch was being dutifully swept. At the village shop, the friendly shopkeeper came out to croon at Meg. We were surrounded by builder's rubble, and she proudly informed me that they would have their own cafe shortly. This I could scarcely grasp, since this island of enterprise was already the village grocery, post office and hairdresser! I left Rockcliffe on a high road above the river, with fine views south-west back to the Lake District. I tried in vain to spot the monument to King Edward I on Burghmarsh at Edenmouth, the scene of his death. The Hammer of the Scots and schemer of the *ring of stone* against the Welsh died of dysentery on a *three degree* saltmarsh. We crossed estate lands of plantations and game birds, of screeching jays, clattering woodpigeons and silly, startled pheasants. Ahead were the major Anglo-Scottish communication arteries, the A74 trunk road and the west-coast railway. Annan power station cooling towers were visible, a sure sign of home and Scotland. I felt a rush of blood as I realised that the Scottish border was close at hand — this would be a significant point in the walk.

I had to cross the railway line, which I did with due caution and trepidation. It was busy, and electric trains and even high speed 125s were whizzing by. Apparently there were problems on the east-coast line, which explained the appearance of the 125s. One mystery was solved as I passed through Metal Bridge. I had always wondered as I drove by on the A74 why Metal Bridge should be so named. A plaque underneath the road bridge explained that its name derived from a metal bridge erected over the Esk in 1820, which has since been replaced with the trunk road bridge. Obvious, but true. Major route changes were enforced ahead, by the absence of a bridge over the River Lyne. I had intended to go by way of Longtown to Scotsdike. But a bridge marked on the map definitely does not exist, which led to a reshuffle of my route, and I crossed the Esk by the side of screaming juggernauts and whining cars over the Concrete Bridge. This was an unfortunate and unpleasant experience, particularly since I had to continue alongside the trunk road for a further two miles into Gretna. I used the old road, I speeded up, I did everything possible to make those two miles disappear faster. It was the most unpleasant two miles of the whole trip, with the reward of arriving at the Scottish border at the River Sark in Gretna. By the time Norman came to retrieve me I was already smiling again.

# Part V     The Scottish Borders

# The Queen o' Meg' Dale

## Gretna Green to Meggat Water

Under Scots law in the early nineteenth century it was possible for young couples to marry without parental consent from the age of sixteen. South of the border, though, without consent, couples had to wait until they had come of age, at twenty-one years. Because of this discrepancy Gretna Green became famous the world over. Runaway couples, often chased by angry parents, fled north to Scotland to be married. The old blacksmith's shop and the toll bar were the first buildings encountered once over the border. Thus they were the scene of over 20,000 marriages, and one 'anvil priest' alone, Richard Rennison, conducted 5,147. The blacksmith would often knock up villagers in the dead of night to act as witnesses to the marriages. Subsequent changes in the marriage laws have reduced the weddings at Gretna to zealots only, and the ceremonial buildings have succumbed to the tartan, trinkets and tweed of the tourist trade — but not overnight. The old blacksmith's shop was opened to the public for the first time in 1887, so it's into its second century as a tourist attraction.

It was not until July, several weeks on into the summer, that I

The first house in Scotland, Gretna Green.

A grasshopper warbler
in the hedgerow
reeling its curious
fishing-reel song
*— Gretna.*

was able to resume *three degrees* and stand before the tartan regalia of the old blacksmith's shop in a dull light under a heavy sky. It was about to rain. Inside the shop, assistants heavily outnumbered the odd German tourist. I was assured by the leaflet that the piper would play me a welcome, but he was indifferent to the point of dragging on a cigarette. Sure enough, a coach appeared out of the murk, and he was transformed into a bullfrog of air. I left this tourist honeypot to the sound of 'Glencoe' above the traffic of the A74. For a few minutes, the heavens opened.

I crossed the railway again. Now the herbage in the hedgerows was taller than me: grasses, vetches, crosswort and dog rose. I walked right past a grasshopper warbler in the hedgerow reeling its curious fishing-reel song. My horizons were limited by these hedgerow lanes. It was green and pastoral, and didn't feel particularly Scottish. England was still only less than a mile away, for we were walking parallel with the border river Sark. Honeysuckle and meadowsweet dripped with scent and raindrops. A curlew's delicious warble in the air over an island of rough teased my ears. A youngster sped by on a BMX bike and shouted 'hello'. An old grey Austin A7 van passed slowly by, and time stood still.

A mile away, across the Sark on Solway Moss, is the site of a victorious English battle of 1542. Henry VIII's forces inflicted a heavy defeat on James V's weary army of 10,000 Scots. It was less than thirty years since Henry VIII had last delivered a mortal blow to Scotland at Flodden, when James IV and much of the Scottish nobility were killed. As it was, Solway Moss left James V a broken man, and he died only three weeks after the rout, at his palace of Falkland in Fife. His compensation was that a mere week before he died, his wife, Mary of Guise, bore him an heir, one of the most charismatic figures of Scottish history: Mary Queen of Scots.

Campingholm farmstead had a round byre, or horse gin, and a scatter of Muscovies and a cockerel. I recrossed the Sark back into England for a couple of miles, before making Scotland for good. Englishtown farmstead was indeed an outpost of England, and, despite its quaint name, was a tribute to modern farming, with slurry tanks, steel outsheds and a kit bungalow around the original steading. The Scotsdike, an ancient earthwork, held the immediate horizon. By a gap in the Scotsdike, half a dozen guinea fowl provided a perfect border watch, and ran towards Meg chattering in unison. The earthwork was so named following an Anglo-Scottish treaty of 1552 when the border was moved from the Esk to the Sark. A barrier — the Scotsdike — was constructed between the two rivers.

The rain was intermittent and led to the frustrating donning and shedding of waterproofs. Freshly cut swathes of silage patterned the landscape into an athletic track for tractors. I began to traverse rougher ground. Poorly drained areas became the domain of rashes and pink ragged robin. Curlews shrieked overhead and their cries echoed across the muirs. Whinchats and meadow pipits flickered on the barbed wire fences like punctuation marks along a sentence. Two kestrels sped away.

Somewhere between Hagg Hill and Kerr Height my armchair planning went awry and the muir became trackless and soaking wet. It held a massive bull with his harem of cows and their calves. As bad luck would have it, the bull was directly *en route*, track or no track. I had committed myself to a vast open muir,

Whinchats flickered on
the barbed wire fence
like punctuation marks
in a sentence
  *– Hagg Hill.*

and to skirt this monster required a major detour. He was not popular. My biggest problem was Meg, for cows in general dislike dogs; and cows with calves are not creatures to upset, and in reality are far more dangerous than bulls. I stopped well in advance of this lot and decided upon a course of action. My plan was to skirt the hazard, giving as little ground away as possible, since I had a way to go and wished to conserve my energy. Good. Decision made, I moved left, to the west. It became obvious fairly quickly that the cows had spotted my movements, and, much worse, had spotted Meg. Anxiously I searched for the bull — he was moving with the pack. I looked around in earnest for possible means of escape, but by this time I had committed myself absolutely to the muir. I increased pace to a quick walk. So did the cows. I began to half-walk, half-run. So did the cows. By now they were less than a hundred metres away and gaining. I began to run. So did the cows. Suddenly I realised that the cows had split and I was carrying a splinter group away with me, without the bull. In addition, they seemed content to run parallel to us. Relieved, I slowed down and calmed down. Meg thought it great fun for she enjoys running! But it was a scare in my book, and next time I'll choose a wider berth. Shortly afterwards I abandoned this plod over the muir, and cut east through some forest plantations onto the A7. I was happy this time to swap cows for cars, and followed the main road along the River Esk into Langholm. Somewhere along the roadside I noted the gory sight of forty moles strung up along the fence.

Langholm is an industrial mill town on the Esk, and the chimneys and neat rows of terraced houses reminded me of the

Dark satanic mills,
Langholm.

Lancashire towns of my youth. It was raining, which also
brought back memories of childhood. The villas of the wealthy
sat high over the town. I walked along the west bank of the Esk,
opposite the main road, along a pleasant track through
farmland, woodland and a town park. Street names in Langholm
spoke of its connections — Buccleuch Square and Thomas
Telford Road. We passed the Academy, and crossed the Esk by a
metal estate bridge, admiring the many small trout which darted
in the river below, and wandered into parkland.

By a bend in the river lay an enormous rearing system for
pheasant poults, with dozens of pens lit and heated by gas units.
A four wheel drive motor-cycle was parked with a trailer loaded
to the gunwales with pheasant-rearing pellets. Undoubtedly this
is big business, though I will never understand why. I met an
elderly couple along a forest track, and we exchanged greetings
and (un)pleasantries regarding the weather. I imagined that they
were the owners of the estate, they were so well spoken and
eccentrically dressed. She sported an ancient umbrella and
raincoat, whilst the laird had on a waxed jacket and old round
bone spectacles. Flies surrounded the pair of them, and he
remarked that he was 'just as hot inside'. I hurried on lest the
flies found me.

At Potholm I investigated a cemetery before climbing a burn
onto the road on Golf Hill, and entering Westerhall estate. A
mausoleum celebrated the lairds at Kirktonhill, with the macabre

carving of a cow skull on the outside. Its domed roof glistened with rain, and a tablet explained the history of the building: erected in 1824 in memory of John Johnstone of Alva, 4th son of Sir James Johnstone of Westerhall (1734-1795). Too early for Sir James Johnstone of Celtic Park. I was more interested in the gravestones of the shepherds of Westerhall, and discovered one Andrew Little who died in 1697, almost three hundred years ago.

Eskdale was enjoyable in the gentle bleating of the early evening, and even the rain stopped. Dykes are constructed hereabouts with very small stones, giving a distinct upland character. Yellow lava flows of buttercups coloured the braes. Many small conifer belts had been planted, sewing a pleasant patchwork on the hillsides. I had yet to reach the endless conifer forests of Eskdalemuir and the borders. By now I was weary and footsore, and camped at the confluence of Stennies Water with Meggat Water. I attempted to pitch the tent, and discovered that I had forgotten the tent poles! An immediate search for wooden poles led to a jury-rigged tent. Meg of Meg'dale appeared suitably regal, once she had eaten her supper. It soon became apparent that I was in Scotland at last, since the midges were fearsome. Meg knocked over a mug of tea as she encircled a rabbit that she had trapped under a pile of logs. I banished the queen o' Meg'dale to the rear of the tent in disgrace. Struggling with tired eyes and a book, Paul Theroux's *Journey Around Britain*, far too cynical even for a trusty campaigner like myself, I turned in and slept deliciously well.

# 21  Border Forests

## Meggat Water to Kingside Loch

It took the alarm to rouse me at eight. Outside the tent came the natural alarm calls of the crows and the more distant cheeps of the dippers of Meggat Water. Tuesday began bright, but with much moisture in the sky. We headed due north for a slow pull up the dale. A hare shot off, and calling Meg to heel, I watched its flight. As it sprinted away it lowered its ears at regular intervals, keeping them alert most of the time. As we gained height, the alder fringe to the water ended, as did the hay and silage fields, and so the uplands advanced. A rain squall enhanced their advance. Wheatears delivered their scratchy tunes from the dykes, and oystercatchers guarded stones in the river with noisy shrieks.

A motorist stopped for a chat. He belonged to Edinburgh, but spent several holidays a year up the glen at Jamestown, and had researched its history. Meg'dale had been a populous area at one time, in common with much of rural Scotland, with a school and a library. In the past antimony had been mined here, a metal which has special properties as it expands rather than contracts upon cooling. It was much in demand in the nineteenth century for the print industries and for medical purposes. With the passing of the mining, the area's prosperity declined, and depopulation followed.

Megdale House was charmingly urbane, nestling in a copse. It had a neat wheelbarrow complete with red trimmings beneath the window, and an immaculate garden. A porcelain dog adorned a window. Guinea fowl chattered angrily at our passing, and a half-dozen domestic geese blustered away at us. I discovered a faded chimneysweeper moth on the roadside. These are beautiful creatures in their prime, and are aptly named small dark moths with white edgings on their wings, about the size of the blue butterflies. They feed on the pignut flowers, and are seen in early summer. Both black-headed and lesser black-backed gulls patrolled their glen which filled with noise. Orange balsam, known as monkey flowers, decorated the waterside.

I passed what certainly had been the old schoolhouse. Change and modernisation were approaching even this upland cul-de-sac, and the old-fashioned 'cattle grid' signs were doomed, pending replacement with modern red triangle signs lying in wait on the roadside. Yellow paint and arrows on the tarmac gave the game away. A feeling of excitement swept over me as I saw a rough track in the distance climb northwards. I turned a corner and civilised Meg'dale was gone. Ahead was a broad glaciated sweep of coarse grasses and bracken, with an enormous forest on the horizon. Angular, newly shorn sheep shivered away and a pair of kestrels circled overhead: *kekka-kekka-kekka-kekka*. I was in my beloved uplands again, and just to prove it had to restore a couped sheep to its feet on the trackside. A lamb nestled against her side out of the wind. I heaved mum over and onto her feet, and held her fast for as long as I was able, for she was heavy and with full fleece. It's best to keep them held in an upright position for a couple of minutes, until the circulation is restored to their legs. Without this precaution they frequently tumble over again, the saturated fleece causing the imbalance. My hands now stank of lanolin.

It started to rain heavily as I entered the forest, smelling of pine and spruce. Only three months ago I had been in the company of one of the minders of these border forests, Economic Forestry Group's Wildlife Manager, Ronnie Rose. Anyone involved in wildlife or countryside management in Scotland encounters Ronnie Rose sooner or later. Ronnie is a larger-than-life character, the son of a Balmoral keeper, who spent over twenty years as a ranger with the Forestry Commission in the Trossachs. He has been at Eskdalemuir for twenty years, and provides a colourful presence in his three-piece stalking tweed, or kilt, depending on the occasion. Solidly built and around sixty years of age, he has the ruddy face of an outdoor man; he is ebullient, some would say arrogant, yet his genuine love of Scotland somehow wins the day. At Eskdalemuir he has skilfully managed the wildlife in over 150 square kilometres, such that raptors and passerines are common in what is essentially a coniferous forest, which are usually wildlife deserts. He has ensured that wildlife corridors remain in the forest, by the judicious planting of broadleaves along burnsides and rides, and he manages his roe deer population with great care. In this way, kestrels, short-eared owls and buzzards are common. Merlin, peregrine and sparrowhawk are also present. Many keepers would raise an eyebrow, or even a shotgun (despite the law) at this, but Ronnie's arguments show the way forward. He insists that farmers, foresters and conservationists have to learn to live with each others' views, and this can be achieved through sympathetic wildlife management. Many foresters would certainly cringe at an estimated population of 1,500 roe deer in the forest. Roe deer can wreak havoc by eating trees and can cause damage by brashing with their antlers. Ronnie's team of rangers cull about a third each year, and diligently maintain the territories of the dominant bucks, who ensure that the younger bucks are kept out of the forest. Similar theories have been advocated regarding fox control (not by

Ronnie!). There's an equally colourful character in the Trossachs, a shepherd and author by the name of John Barrington, who maintains that the well-established dog fox will keep the troublesome younger foxes from marauding the hefts of the hill. His book about a shepherding year by Loch Katrine, *Red Sky at Night*, is a beautiful piece of writing. Ronnie should write a book, for he has a fund of stories, and a working knowledge of wildlife that is second to none.

The whispering calls of goldcrests accompanied the abrasive rasps of the chaffinches in the forest. Foxgloves and heath bedstraw provided a splash of colour, purple and white. I passed an old quarry where two hares were chasing each other — one came so close that I felt the ground pounded by its feet. Conical cypresses stood at the forest edge like giant chessmen.

We wandered through an area of recently cleared softwoods, and even spotted some tree tubes, signifying a replant of broadleaves. This bleak expanse was the domain of meadow pipits, and wrens which hurried through the brash. A dark speck over the big hills to westward was a buzzard, which in the poor light I had at first thought was an eagle. Two single roe deer lolloped away. Lunch was taken behind a small remnant plantation, fending off midges and rain. We crossed the threshold via Stock Hill and began the descent to Craik, looking in vain for an unplanted area shown on the map. It had been planted, so I took the new tracks and rides, through waist-high grass and thistles. I was wet through in no time at all, and sought compensation and delight in the names of the old settlements: Howpasley Hope, Old Howpasley and, of course, Howpasley itself. Hope had run out for the highest and first encountered Howpasley, for it was a ruin, and a great contrast to Old Howpasley, a fine building with a byre. House martins were swooping along the river, glinting in the sun. The rain had stopped and I had found a track. Things were looking up. Yellow flags adorned the river, setting off the symmetry of the Roman road to Craik.

I had a leisurely passage through the Forestry Commission village of Craik, and phoned home from a box with a neat floral border which was fondly cared for by a local. An old, blind retriever came sniffing, doubtless scenting Meg. By Craik farm and the Aithouse Burn I drummed up, wrung out my socks, and began to enjoy the change of weather and the hot sun. Bonnie purple marsh orchids studded the grass. Instead of taking an easier route along a major forest track, I followed a smaller trail, dappled with light through the conifers, and was rewarded by seeing a pair of bullfinches. When I took up the main track I was rewarded by seeing a Ford Fiesta!

After a nine-hour day I called a halt, at Kingside Loch, and set about a search for tent poles – no shortage of brashings in the

Yellow flags, at
Howparsley Burn,
Craik Forest.

Jury-rigged camp,
Kingside Loch.

forest! Tufted duck and coot sailed on the lochan. About an hour later I heard the unmistakable sound of a Landrover engine, and the equally distinctive noise of its doors being slammed. Two folk, a man and a woman, had come to fish. The midges were unbearable and I realised that Meg was not safely housed in the tent. I discovered her rolling in the forest, covered in a seething mass of midges. If one can imagine a trillion midges in the shape of a dog, this was it. Quickly, I brushed her down with my hands, and we dived into the tent. Only a quarter of a million midges came with us, to cause annoyance for some time. Outside the tent, on my walking boot, an orange-coloured fly actually stalked, pounced upon, and ate several midges. This surely was a friend, but I only saw the one . . .

A most beautiful sunset followed, of gold and purple clouds. Fish splashed in the loch. Around ten in the evening, the fisherman came over and asked in a plum voice whether I had permission to camp. My reply was polite enough, but sufficiently informed and succinct. I had an idea that I was on Forestry Commission property, that no-one would ever know that I had been there, and that I would be away at first light. He pursued his point enough to enquire whether I intended to fish. I replied that I didn't intend to leave the tent. I guessed that he was attempting to prove something to his female acquaintance, or perhaps he was genuinely concerned about the fishery. Either way, he was having obvious problems with the midges while trying to hold a conversation with an unknown quantity inside a tent who was not having trouble with the midges (little did he know!). As he stood outside waving his arms like a lunatic I think that he got my point. So I asked him whether he had had any luck, and let vanity do the rest. 'Just one small one,' he replied, 'that's fine.' Did he mean my camping, or the fish? He let it rest with an upper-class grunt, and Meg vented her feelings about the matter with a few growls and even a bark or two. She rarely barks, but dislikes upper-class twits and midges.

# 22 Traquair and Tweed

## Kingside Loch to Innerleithen

A misty July morning, broken only by the calls of willow warblers, the trill of a little grebe on the lochan, and an aircraft overhead. A solitary hawthorn cast its scent over the tent; here the May is in July.

I returned to the old routine of tramping forest rides, through a profusion of pignut on their edges, but no chimneysweepers remained. It was like walking through a giant maze in the countryside, for the trees gave little away of the distance, and one's horizon was severely limited. Even at an early hour I decided that I'd had enough and declared myself psychologically debilitated. I passed signs for the Goose and Windylaw Lochs, and some freshly cut thinnings brought a sense of relief and proportion to the view through the trees of the Crooked Loch. Later, a fisherman approached on the track, a youth in his early twenties, dressed in fisher-green from head to toe. I stopped him for a chat, and asked where he was headed — the Goose Loch. He told me that Kingside Loch was private, and well watched, and wasn't surprised at my encounter with officialdom. We parted, and the forest was silent again.

Subliminally the forest conquered me, and I took a wrong turn, my concentration having lapsed. Moreover, it was a mile before I appreciated the error, by sensing a change in the movement of the clouds, and being unable to recognise the northward land features between forest rides. I was annoyed with myself. I had wished myself out of the forest but instead had succeeded in adding two miles onto the day. It was my only navigational blunder of the whole trip (I still maintain that the fracas in the field near Arthur's Stone was on a public footpath!), and once more I had been tricked by a big forest. I remember an occasion as a teenager in the company of two friends in Culbin Forest in Morayshire when we got ourselves lost. It was the only day we didn't have a compass with us, and ultimately we had to scale a tree to get our position! Every cloud has a silver lining, and my reward for perseverance with the forest was the sight of siskins overhead, identified by their shrill calls and the sun piercing their wingbars. Crossbills also dashed across the ride, these too identified by their call-notes, and heavy heads. Forest wildlife consists of a series of glimpses, and razor-sharp senses are needed to catch the residents as they flit through the tree tops, or bound through the rides.

At last we were free of the forest, and we made a dash for

freedom over the muirs towards Drycleuchlea. This was a large farmhouse with many cars parked outside, so I took a self-imposed detour around some small plantations to the east of the house. Strung up along one of the plantation fences was a dead fox, not unexpected in sheep country, which wore an unpleasant snarl of death. Thunder and lightning began in the east, adding to the aura of grimness. Meg gave a howl as she walked into an electric fence. The muir was getting spooky, and I was uneasy about crossing the open, high expanse, with flashes of fire in the sky. So much for 'safe' walking in Britain, with an encounter with a bull and now lightning to contend with. At the edge of a plantation we sheltered for five minutes from the heavy rain. Satisfied that the lightning was well to the east, we made a dash across the muir, getting atrociously wet in the process. The rain lashed down, and after a mile or so we made the shelter of the ruined shepherd's bothy of Whitehillshiel. Little remained of roof or floorboards, but we found shelter and drummed up. Through the patter of rain, I admired the old cast-iron fireplace, old veterinary bottles for the treatment of sheep ailments, and even an old chemical lavatory. I didn't dare go up the rotten stairase into the rain.

We resumed our quest, through new Tilhill forest plantings, but without a track. I managed to locate a new access track but not before I was wringing wet again. Progress then became easy, especially after I'd changed my socks and removed my waterproofs once the rain had stopped. I descended into the Ettrick Valley, and sang the well-known folk song:

As I gae'd doon the Ettrick Valley
At the hour of twelve at night,
Who did I see but a handsome lassie
Combing her hair by candlelight.

A family of four kestrels followed me down Hyndhope. The hills of the Ettrick Forest loomed large ahead, Sundhope Height in particular. Hyndhope Farm and its satellite cottages were very attractive, but had nets flailing from the eaves, presumably in an attempt to prevent the house martins nesting. No countryman would ever think of such a trick, and I snorted in disgust on behalf of the martins. Vapour rose from the wet road courtesy of the hot sun. Walking along the Ettrick into a light breeze was very pleasant, into the scent of the meadowsweet and lady's bedstraw. A shepherd was working his dogs on the hill, and his whistles and oaths mingled with the scent of the wildflowers. Ettrickside was mottled with the meandering shadows of the storm clouds, chasing the river down the glen.

I was sorely tempted by the thought of a lunchtime pint at the Ettrickshaws Country House Hotel, but it involved a slight detour and was probably too exclusive for an itinerant and his dog. Ettrick, for all its loveliness, seemed conservative, all farming, fishing and country house hotels. I turned northward again by the shattered perpendicular crags over the river at Kirkhope, towards the Old Kirkhope tower on the hill. I took more tea by a humpbacked bridge overlooking the tower.

High over Witchie Knowe I looked back at Ettrick, and was struck once more by the beauty of the landscape. Beneath me, a couple of circular sheep fanks with drystane-dyke tails were like giant sperms on the hillside. The huge forests of my route now well in the distance looked much less menacing. We crossed the watershed and entered the domain of the Yarrow. At once, the impressive whaleback of Hare Law and Brown Knowe dominated the horizon. They also carry the route of an old drove road from Tweed to Ettrick. Patches of burned heather, shooting butts, and circular plantations neatly enclosed by drystane dykes all indicated a well-managed landscape. We crossed the Yarrow and headed up a glen towards Welldean Hill. Walking was hard, but exciting and panoramic, crossing the historic rivers of Ettrick, Yarrow and Tweed. Above an alder-fringed gorge it became excessively hot and I called a halt to feed Meg. Sheep fanks dotted the hillside, and partridge calls filled the air. On Welldean Hill a strange series of barrow-like cairns followed the slope; there were at least five, about two metres long by one metre in height. I was going slowly enough to admire the hill flowers — tormentil, thyme, heath bedstraw and mountain violets.

On the summit of Glengaber, I experienced one of those sublime moments. A strong wind was blowing from the west, and I was surrounded by rounded peak upon rounded peak. It began to rain hard as a black squall hit, driving horizontally at our backs. In less than five minutes the tumult had passed, and the sun steamed us dry again. It was fantastic. Innerleithen was distant, tantalising and glinting in the sunlight behind the dark forests of Traquair. We contoured around the hillside and entered the forest. By following the forest tracks I had lost some height which I recaptured with some hardship. It was that stage when overdrive takes over, and the miles of the winding forest track fell quickly away. My first view of the Tweed, over Traquair House, with the hillside and Iron Age fort of Lee Pen above, was one of the most memorable of the whole trip. The Scottish borders had provided magnificent wild walking, and a mile or two later I crossed the route of the more *official* wild walk, the Southern Upland Way. This was Britain's first east–west, coast-to-coast long-distance footpath, and runs for 212 miles from Portpatrick to Cockburnspath. Innerleithen was suddenly very close. A huge black and white mill dominated the town. We crossed the Tweed and passed the old toll house by the brig, dated 1830. Bunting fluttered in the streets, and I wondered why there was all this fuss for our arrival. It transpired that the Queen had visited recently, and had stayed overnight nearby. Scott popularised the town in *St Ronan's Well,* his novel named after its patron saint. It was a spa town as well as a textile centre, and remains a centre for knitwear. Other remnants in the town are the unusual London street names — The Strand, Piccadilly, Bond Street — a legacy of the Earl of Traquair. We met Kate and rounded off a successful trip with a fish supper and a couple of beers, but not, I'm ashamed to admit, Traquair House ale. Traquair claims to be the oldest continually inhabited house in Scotland. It has been lived in since the twelfth century, and has changed little since the seventeenth-century additions. Mary Queen of Scots stayed there, but where didn't she? The brewery came much later, indeed not until the eighteenth century. Traquair's original entrance was locked by the laird after Bonnie Prince Charlie had passed through in the '45. He declared that the gate would remain locked until a Stewart regained the throne of Britain. It remains locked to this day.

# 23　Gala Water

## Walkerburn to Prestonpans

From Tweed to Forth was to prove an epic walk of around thirty-two miles, in the company of Donald Gunn, a friend and artist who has captured the wildlife of *three degrees* throughout these pages. We left the Tweed at Walkerburn and ascended Gatehopeknowe burn, bypassed its lower defences of pheasant pens and gundog kennels, and climbed its incised course towards the rolling hills of the Moorfoots. A pair of hunters emerged from a secondary glen, and made for a small tent which had been neatly erected in a paddock, and bore such trappings as empty wine bottles and a barbecue stand. This combination was too much for Donald who suggested that they might be out shooting campers! Hares gambolled away — perhaps more appropriate quarry — and kestrels patrolled overhead. Seathope cottage, we agreed, would prove a wonderful retreat in the hills, nestling in trees at the head of a fork in the burns. As I photographed an old meat trailer which now appropriately served as a sheep shelter, a weasel darted cross our path. We contoured out of the glen and onto the summit plateau which was exposed and windy. Windlestraw Law yielded extensive views of the distinctive Eildon Hills to the south-east, and of Edinburgh and the Lomonds of Fife to the north. Moorfoot

Meat trailer, Seathope.

Golden provers whistled plaintively at us – *The Moorfoot Hills.*

heather rolled around us and we were in a swell of summits.

At first the plateau seemed bleak and lifeless, but just as one's eyes become accustomed to the dark, so we became accustomed to the muir. We strode through carpets of thick cloudberry leaves, peat hags and heather. It wasn't easy going, but the rewards were just. Golden plovers whistled plaintively at us; mountain hares stood erect and watched our passing; and occasionally the heather would explode as a family of grouse careered away, the youngsters with barely a tail. Pipits fluttered and called constantly. Without doubt the star of the show was a dunlin in summer plumage, with a perfect black belly, a soft *creech creech* call, and a successful delicate flight into a torrent of wind. We also disturbed snipe, though their powerful zig-zag escape flight is far from delicate, any more than their harsh call.

By Dod Law, Moorfoot Hills.

With the grouse came the shooting butts, recessed and dug out of the hill for novelty. George Wood, at 500 metres on the windswept plateau, was too inhospitable a place to expect any trees to flourish. They didn't. A fire had swept the plantation, and the skeletons of trees produced an image of warfare. Those trees which had survived the wind grew only in miniature, such that the Scots pines had a mature shape yet were only ten feet high, like a natural bonsai plantation. Some trees which had been the victim of windthrow were regrowing branches from a prostrate position.

By now we were enjoying immediate views of the Pentland range, to the south-east of Edinburgh, and could clearly see the volcanic plateau of the Lomonds of Fife. These are extinct volcanoes and have distinctive conical shapes. We arrived at a track which would lead us down to Gala Water, and changed into more comfortable training shoes, since we still had over twenty miles to walk. Splendid mature sycamore and beech lined our track, and fields full of ripening barley rippled in the breeze. Rooks and magpies were strung up along the fencelines. Corsehope Pools held some teal and mallard and the burn took us between two Iron Age settlements. We crossed Gala Water and hummed the Burns tune:

Braw, braw lads on Yarrow braes,
They rove amang the blooming heather;
But Yarrow braes nor Ettrick shaws
Can match the lads o' Gala Water.

Shoestanes Terrace was a small collection of council houses in

Shepherd's shed,
Shoestanes, Moorfoot
Hills.

the middle of nowhere! Along a track nearby a shepherd's crook
hung by a shed doorway giving a clue as to the livelihood of
its resident. Across the barley fields the Pentlands appeared
massive, yet the Lomonds in the distance remained their great
rivals. As we rested by a brig at Middleton, an old boy out
from Dalkeith engaged us in conversation. He spoke of
walking these lanes in the Depression of the '30s, in much the
same way as climbers from Glasgow foraged into the southern
Highlands. He informed us that we'd been walking the course of

Italian renaissance interior, Crichton Castle, Vale of Tyne, Lothian.

an old coach road across from Shoestanes, and that his childhood had been spent evading the keepers among the muirs and gorse. 'There's been some changes,' he concluded, and wished us well on our route to the Pans. Middleton Hall estate had been transformed into a children's camp, and the parkland lay occupied by soccer and rugby pitches and dormitories. We found ourselves trapped in the estate, and had to scale a wall to escape.

Amidst the castle and church towers of history, Currie Mains seemed to be an Edinburgh stockbrokers' retreat. We passed a scout camp and a horsy concern. A wonderful oakwood, now a Woodland Trust property, gave an inspiring lead into the realm of Crichton Castle. Scott was right about Crichton, in that the castle rises steeply from the green vale of Tyne. It was the family seat of Lord Crichton from the thirteenth to fifteenth centuries; and of the Earls of Bothwell until the end of the sixteenth century. The first Lord Crichton, Sir William, was one of its most influential lairds. He was governor of Scotland during the young King James II's minority, and later chancellor. Crichton's bitter rivals were the Black Douglases from Kirkcudbrightshire. At the celebrated Black Dinner of 1440 in Edinburgh Castle, Crichton had two heirs of the Douglas Family murdered in front of James II, after a bull's head had been placed on the table to signify their doom. It was the third Lord Crichton who forfeited the estate after a series of scandals and conspiracies. The Bothwell era was almost as brief, and the castle was rarely at the centre stage of their exploits. James, the fourth earl, was the third husband of Mary Queen of Scots. It was the fifth earl, however, Francis Stewart, in the 1580s who had a profound influence on the castle. Stewart was a wild man, at once a ruffian and man of culture, who was repeatedly forced abroad to Italy and Spain because of his schizophrenia. This Latin influence has resulted in a unique diamond-faceted courtyard. Crichton's aspect is impressive, occupying its steep knoll with the smaller stable block, and yet it is this Italian Renaissance interior which steals the show.

Crichton's significance did not end with the castle, for a sign outside the kirk reads 'Church of Scotland Crichton Historic Scottish Kirk'. It is a seventeenth-century former collegiate church, dedicated to St Mary and St Kentigern. Originally we had intended to traverse the Vogrie estate, now a Country Park, but we were losing time and couldn't find a convenient access point, so instead we continued to the Preston Hall estate beyond Pathhead village. Its impressive wrought-iron gateway supported two white lion sentinels, although its lodge house was boarded up and empty. Set in the parkland were some magnificent chestnut, beech, copper beech and Chilean pine trees. A herd of bullocks chased us through a field such that our view of a temple set on the edge of the park was fleeting.

Here was a countryside of contrasts, of estate parkland and pit bings of the Lothian coalfield near Ormiston; of the tiny chapel of Elphinstone (measuring only twelve metres by ten); and the medieval mansionhouse castles at Elphinstone and Fa'side. We wove northwards by means of disused railway tracks, now nature trails, footpaths and minor roads. A mile or so to the west of our route along the railway track and Elphinstone Tower lies Carberry Hill and a site known as Queen Mary's Mount. This was the scene of Mary Queen of Scots' and her third husband the Earl of Bothwell's confrontation with the rebel confederate Lords, who held her son James (later VI of Scotland and I of England). Mary had turned to Bothwell after the murder of her lover Rizzio by Darnley, her second husband. Darnley was then murdered in a Scottish equivalent of the Gunpowder Plot, when the house in Edinburgh in which he was staying was blown up, Bothwell being implicated in the explosion. Darnley did in fact escape the explosion but was killed outside. Bothwell was a powerful East Lothian landowner with many castles (including Crichton) and Mary considered him strong enough to further her cause and rescue her monarchy and son. He was also a notorious womaniser and was hardly likely to refuse her! In any event, Bothwell kidnapped Mary, some say with her prior knowledge of the plot, and forced her to marry him. Bothwell then raised an army of some 2,000 local followers and marched with the Queen towards the capital. At Carberry Hill the two sides met, and much argument ensued between the leaders whilst the Confederates strengthened their position around the hill. Mary's army fled and left her to her fate – imprisonment in Loch Leven castle, and escape to England and eventual execution. Bothwell fled to Norway via Orkney, and died a madman in a Danish prison. Mary's son was eventually to unite the Crowns of Scotland and England for the first time.

A last climb of the day led us past Fa'side Castle onto Falside Hill for what should have been a commanding view over Edinburgh and the Forth, but this was denied by the worsening visibility and fading light. Fa'side Castle had certainly been situated with defence in mind and is a splendid example of a laird's tower-house. In the turbulent Middle Ages, it was essential for large landowners to have some form of protection against the constant threat of attack. Civil wars, wars against the English, religious feuds and the Jacobite campaigns meant that fortified tower-houses, a cheaper version of a castle, became common in lowland Scotland. In East Lothian alone, in the space of four miles, we were to walk past three fine examples — Elphinstone Tower, Fa'side Castle, and Preston Tower. These towers are frequently at the centre of estates, a testimony to their domestic nature. Both Elphinstone and Fa'side command strategic views, and it is ironic that the fifteenth-century Elphinstone Tower survived the onslaughts of time, only to be ruined by mining subsidence. Many towers, including Fa'side, had a prison since those with barony status had rights at the lowest level of law enforcement. Successful landowners often added to their relatively cramped towers, and Fa'side was doubled in size in the sixteenth century by adding a wing. A novel way of increasing size was undertaken at Preston Tower, which still has a double-decker appearance.

In later years, as the coalfields developed, Lady Fa'side persuaded the wealthy Lothian coalmasters, in a price-fixing ring of 1620, to illegally raise the price of coal and thereby hinder the Scottish government's attempts to curb inflation. Some things don't change. The National Trust for Scotland restored the castle in 1982, but there seems little hope of restoring the Lothian coalfield. Its story, and the story of Scottish coal, is told by the Scottish Mining Museum which has a centre based on the Prestongrange beam engine at Prestonpans. Fife was barely visible across the Forth as we descended into the Pans. In the gloom we could see the twin towers of Cockenzie power station and the long, symmetrical sweep of the Forth across Musselburgh and Leith, culminating in the Forth road and rail bridges. Inchkeith island stood in the firth, familiar by its lighthouse. With an uncanny sense of timing, it began to rain just as we entered Prestonpans.

Preston village and Prestonpans exude history! Preston Tower holds one's attention because of its strange additional tower above the original parapet walk. The village also boasts what is perhaps the finest mercat cross in Scotland, although it's not a cross at all but an early seventeenth-century rotunda which incorporates seats, doors and a platform in its design. Its shaft is topped by a unicorn which has presided over markets ever since the first one held in 1617. It is battles, however, with which one associates Prestonpans, for there have been two significant clashes within a three-mile radius. Beneath Fa'side Castle lies the battlefield of Pinkie. Henry VIII had invaded Scotland in 1544–45 in order to try and force the Scots to agree to the marriage of his son Edward to the infant Mary. This became known as the Rough Wooing, and the battle which followed in 1547 as Black Saturday, since almost 12,000 inexperienced and badly led Scots were killed by the Duke of Somerset, or drowned in the Esk whilst trying to escape. Prior to the battle the English had camped on *three degrees* on Fa'side Hill.

A more celebrated battle even than Pinkie was that of Prestonpans in 1745, part of Bonnie Prince Charlie's Jacobite rising. The Stewarts had lost their throne in 1689 because the Protestant William of Orange had led a successful 'invasion by invitation' of England, leading to the exile of James VII and II. Several Jacobite rebellions then occurred in Scotland as the Stewarts, with French assistance, pursued their claim to the throne. It was the fourth such rebellion in 1745 which has captured our imagination more than the rest. To begin with there was the occasion of the Prince's landing in Scotland and the gathering of the clans at Glenfinnan. In addition, it almost succeeded, and Charles Edward Stewart led his rebels as far south as Derby, causing Londoners to panic and precipitating a run on the Bank of England. Lastly, there was the final Jacobite defeat at Culloden, and the flight of Prince Charles through the Highlands and Islands, and his escape from the redcoats with Flora Macdonald. At Prestonpans the Jacobites scored their first major victory of the '45 over Sir John Cope. Cope had chased Charlie all over the Highlands and had just disembarked at Dunbar. His men and horses were weary and sick. The Jacobites used a local man to guide them through the marsh protecting the Hanoverians' south flank, and in a surprise attack routed Cope's forces.

> It was upon an afternoon,
> Sir Johnnie march'd to Preston town,
> He says, 'My lads come lean you down,'
> And we'll fight the boys in the morning.'
>
> Hey! Johnnie Cope, are ye wauking yet?
> Or are ye sleeping I would wit;
> O, haste ye get up, for the drums do beat;
> O fye! Cope rise in the morning.

Of local interest to the story was the laird of Bankton House, Colonel Gardiner, leader of Cope's dragoons, who fell in the battle in sight of his own home. Donald, Meg and I had walked by his ruined home, south of Prestonpans station. A monument in the grounds commemorates his fall.

Prestonpans on a Saturday evening was lively, continuing its tradition of battles, with a liberal police presence. In the space of two or three miles we witnessed two marital disputes on the streets. The bars were caverns of noise which burst outside when a door was opened. Donald and I were in no mood for domestic disputes — we had walked a long way on a satisfying route — Kate and Bryony were quite safe . . . and Meg was already fast asleep.

# Part VI    The Scottish Lowlands

# 24  The Royal and Ancient Kingdom of Fife

## Methil to Wormit

My journey through Fife had special meaning, since until recently I worked in Fife as a countryside ranger. It was very much a home game. I picked up *three degrees* on the dockside at Methil, to the west of the sandy sweep of Largo bay. To begin with the weather was poor, and once more I faced a grey industrial dockland. The architecture of greyness was familiar, of grey cranes and grey high-rise flats. Grey Newport. Grey Liverpool. Grey Methil. Fife differed from the other dockyards on *three degrees* in having a thriving rig yard — for the moment anyway – and rigs queued offshore in the Forth awaiting repair. Apart from *Stridence* being unloaded on the west quay, the docks appeared deserted. Elsewhere the waters remained dark and silent, with an expanse of land at the roadside entrance to the docks awaiting redevelopment as an industrial estate. Forth Harbour Authority remain optimistic, however, and active repairs were being carried out to the dock gates — welders spat their tongues of flame at structures on the quayside, and fresh yellow paint rebelled against the day's mood. Good luck to Methil.

Amusements, coastal Fife.

Retired miner, Sandy
McNeil, industrial
Fife.

Methil power station is tiny by modern standards, but situated
on the mouth of the river it dominates the town of Leven and its
promenade. It forms such an incongruous backdrop to the wee
prom as to be almost farcical. Amusement arcades, shows, stalls
and rides, mothers with children, and children with candy floss
were all dwarfed by it. This is the epitome of Britain, where the
pressure on land is so intense that industry and recreation must
lie side by side. To the north and east of Leven lie the
promenade, the golf course, the expanse of Largo Bay and the

Fife landscape from East Lomond, panorama.

East Neuk fishing villages. To the south and west lie the power station, the docks, industrial Kirkcaldy and what's left of the Fife coalfield. Fife has a reputation for its insular nature, an ancient realm of the Scots kings, a peninsula which is protected even today by modern toll bridges across the Forth and Tay. It is also a region of contrasts, between industry and agriculture, old and new, south and north — in fact, a microcosm of Britain.

Meg and I strolled through Letham Glen park in Leven, which was busy at the height of the season. Notices everywhere forbade dogs to follow the main thoroughfare, since Hercules the bear was in residence. After a tour of the gardens, the putting green, the nature centre (where two craftsmen were demonstrating the art of jewellery-making and weaving), and the children's zoo, we skulked through the park on a lesser track. Hercules was in fact well cooped up in a bus and enclosure. His proud owners ushered visitors through to meet their money-making 'child'. Crowds of people sat on the slope of the amphitheatre awaiting Hercules' performance, and the air was electric with the excited squeals of children and piped music. I hurried up the glen, anxious to be away from the razzamatazz and feeling vaguely sick of the whole business.

134

On our way up the narrow glen a wee boy asked his father if I was the postman, doubtless on account of my red rucksack. This amused me greatly, but not I'm afraid, father. 'No, son, it's not,' he said in a straightforward and resigned fashion.

We climbed out of Letham glen, through pasture and past modern houses with close-cropped tidy lawns set in the countryside. Views of the Forth opened up to the rear. The *long arm of the Largo Law* as a Fife folksong has it, monopolised the eastern horizon. Largo Law dominates Largo Bay, and a retired farmer's wife with youthful brown eyes full of fun told me how she and her pals went up the hill on their pushbikes one Hogmanay. She told me some of the local history, of how the sunken garden at Letham Glen was once a swimming pool, and of how the locals still called the park 'Spinky Den' after the name of a local farmer who donated the land to the town. One by one she pointed out the local farms in the landscape and she seemed to have relatives in most. Her husband was just leaving to play golf, and we chatted about the exciting finish to the British Open. The excitement had been too much for his wife who had made a mistake with the quantity of water required for the blackcurrant jam and had created a slop. She fingered a newly

Yellowhammer, Fife.

picked bowl of currants guiltily, and spoke of the 'gowans' (daisies) in the fields and of overgrown tracks. Fife farmers are nothing but friendly.

The tall grasses and exhausted umbellifers gave the hedgerows a faded look. It was not such an attractive countryside: one of chicken houses, kit bungalows and car scrapyards. Wild oats were stacked along the field edges, picked laboriously by unknown hands. We passed beehives and a dozen white geese at Whallyden, and travelled a disused green lane, poorly drained and overgrown with the green and pink tartan of rashes and ragged robin. A young cuckoo flew by, hawk-like and reasonably tame. I chased it along several fence posts before it continued on its amazing journey to Africa, unaccompanied by its parents. We burst through the plantation of Devon Wood to find a panoramic view of the Lomonds of Fife before us. From this angle, both major peaks were directly in line, such that the wireless masts on the summit of East Lomond were hidden by the profile of West Lomond. Fife's contrasts were dramatically exposed from this viewpoint. In front of the Lomonds lay the new town of Glenrothes, now over forty years old, with its urban sprawl and high-rise office blocks. Two abandoned pit heads of Glenrothes colliery stood as memorials to the extinct coalfields, whilst farther west, but no less dominant, lay the petrochemical complex of Mossmorran. The contrast lay to the east of the Lomonds with the Howe (low-lying land) of Fife, a fertile horticultural area, home of Kettle Produce, a large horticultural concern, and Freuchie Cricket Club unlikely (?) winners of the 'national' village championship at that quite essentially English institution, Lords, in 1985.

Road sign, Cupar.

This area is rich farmland. Barley swayed in the breeze and potato fields contained neat flower heads. Linnets, yellowhammers, whitethroats and other finches and warblers were abundant and singing heartily. Scabious, gowans and woundwort lined the hedgerows and field edges with splashes of colour. The major physical changes over recent decades hereabouts have been the loss of many hedgerows, and the arrival of the garish yellow splashes of oilseed rape. We turned a corner and the Hopetoun monument was dead ahead, a prominent landmark of Fife, erected by Fifers in 1827 as a memorial to the 4th Earl. Behind it lay the Scottish Highlands! Progress indeed.

At Chance Inn, a horsy blonde, accompanied by her mount and a grumbling terrier, cursed at the dog and slapped the horse, yet gave me a beaming smile. I smiled back, wondering what I had done to deserve the special treatment. We passed Scotstarvit Tower, a fine example of a seventeenth-century fortified tower built by Sir John Scot, and crossed the busy road into the Hill of Tarvit estate. We conquered the small summit in no time at all, and surveyed the ancient Kingdom beneath us. Fife's old capital and market town of Cupar lay at our feet, to the south-west the Lomonds, to the east the Eden estuary (St Andrews is hidden by the relief), and to the north the Tay and

Agricultural Fife.

Broughty Ferry, east of Dundee. The Sidlaw Hills above Dundee were prominent, but the city of Dundee suffered from the same fate as its university rival, St Andrews. I lay against the monument, and out of the wind. I shooed some cows away, and ran down the hill into Cupar, where I 'phoned home to arrange a pick-up and quaffed a quick glass of lager. The talk in the pub was of duck shooting.

Cupar is a prosperous market town, representative of the contrasts of Fife. It has commanded the Fife agricultural markets since its Royal Charter in the thirteenth century, and was the administrative centre until someone thought of Glenrothes and local government reorganisation. In the town centre is the old mercat cross of 1683, which is in fact the third site that the cross has occupied! It is not dissimilar to the mercat cross at Prestonpans in that it is topped by a unicorn above a rotunda. My interest in the thing stemmed more from my research into the Treaty of Garlie Bank, which I had stumbled into a couple of miles back on the Hill of Tarvit. No one seemed to have heard of this obscure treaty. All was revealed when I discovered that the present monument on Tarvit Hill is a newcomer, dating from Queen Victoria's diamond Jubilee in 1897. Before this, the site (formerly known as Wemyss Hill, after the landowner) had been occupied by Cupar's mercat cross which had been removed from Cupar to save it from the attentions of the vandals. It had been on Wemyss Hill since 1788, placed there to commemorate the treaty signed on the hill in 1559 between the Queen Regent, Marie de Guise-Lorraine, and the Lords of the Congregation — the Treaty of Garlie Bank!

The Tay Bridge from Dundee Law.

We headed quickly through the town and up the hill beyond Hawklaw wireless station. Gardeners at Kingask were picking a plentiful crop of berries as I passed. I spent several frustrating miles walking northwards with no appreciable views, trapped in an upland bowl. In Kilmany village I was astounded by the black life-size statues of a pig and a cat in a garden. One last pull over an old track into Gauldry took me up high at last above the silvery-flowing Tay and Dundee. The Tay bridges were dimly lit by an exhausted sun, and lights began to flicker in the city as the day drew rapidly to a close. We chased the sun, past fields of lettuces, baby leeks, and crates of cabbage plants, and hurried on to Wormit; then by way of a tractor scar in a barley field down to the banks of the Tay.

A breeze followed the course of the river, and courting teenagers walked along the banks. Meg found Kate under the railway bridge, and together we watched a modern 125 slowly cross towards Dundee. This one fared better than the doomed train of 1879 which crossed the bridge in a storm on 28th December. Only two years after the bridge had been opened a structural fault led to its collapse and the train plunged into the Tay with the loss of seventy-five lives. The disaster was of such notoriety that the American President Ulysses S. Grant came to view the scene. When the new bridge opened in 1887 it became the longest bridge in the United Kingdom . . . it still stretches on *three degrees* from Fife to Dundee.

# 25 The Sidlaws

## Dundee to Glen Prosen

It was time for 'the berries', an important time of year for the Carse o' Gowrie, one of the major softfruit-producing areas of Britain. Double-decker buses adorned the raspberry fields, and pickers from Fife, Angus and Tayside plied their way along the arteries of fruit. I was travelling to Dundee, to resume *three degrees*, and as if to emphasise the metaphor, a lorry had disgorged its load of strawberries at the Invergowrie roundabout, and had splattered the road with gore. It had been a bad year for the berries, for the fierce summer storms had battered the fruit.

We resumed *three degrees* on the north-east flank of Dundee. Dundee is a city of ups and doons. Dundee Law and the Observatory Hill are the two prominences of old which now have to compete with the tenements and high-rise blocks, nineteenth- and twentieth-century solutions to the population explosions which the city has experienced. The city remains in the premier league of Scotland's largest cities, but has declined in importance since the seventeenth century when it was second only to the capital. Dundee was formerly a whaling town on the Tay, and has had a turbulent history and changing fortunes through the centuries, its ups and doons proving to be more than physical. Following the flourishing Flemish trade from the fourteenth to the sixteenth centuries, it was devastated by General Monk in 1651, who finally completed what the Vikings, Edward I and Henry VIII had started. John Graham of Claverhouse, 'Bonnie Dundee' himself, even attacked in 1688 as a final irony. Such was the Calvinist fervour of the city during this period that it became known as 'the Geneva of Scotland'. A period of decline and decay followed until the East India Company sent a sample of jute back from Bengal in 1822. Suddenly Dundee was alive again, and an industrial expansion based on jute and linoleum occurred, taking its population from 35,000 in 1836 to 130,000 in 1886. At last Dundee was able to overshadow its traditional rival of Perth, further west along the Tay. Prosperity and the jute barons brought Juteopolis and the wealthy suburbs such as Broughty Ferry. It also brought such alliteration as 'jute, jam and journalism' the jam deriving from Keiller's, founded in 1913, and the presses from D.C. Thomson's journalistic empire. Shipbuilding was an important industry, ever since its whaling origins, and the most famous ship to leave Dundee's yards was undoubtedly Captain R.F. Scott's *Discovery*, the ship on which his ill-fated expedition reached the South

Dundee, city of
*Discovery.*

Pole. *Discovery* served them well, however, and recently the ship was brought home to Tayside, where she now has pride of place on the dock frontage beneath the Tay road bridge. For modern Dundonians she symbolises the rebirth of their city, such that the marketing men have dubbed the place *Dundee — City of Discovery.*

Two Country Parks nestle against each other on this side of the city, Camperdown Park and Templeton Woods, and Clatto. Clatto is a small reservoir site, and does not have the interest of its southerly neighbour, either in habitats or historical associations. Camperdown is a traditional parkland estate of 200 hectares which now includes a golf course, caravan park and riding stables, in addition to the plantations and mansion house designed by William Brown in 1828.

Camperdown was once part of the Lundie Estate of Forfarshire, but its name was changed after the naval battle of Camperdown in 1797, which brought fame to its owner, and the admiral in command of the British fleet, Admiral Adam Duncan, who later became Viscount Duncan of Camperdown and Baron of Lundie. As we strolled through the Country Park on a misty, humid morning, it was difficult to imagine the kind of conditions that the ex-laird would have been accustomed to as an officer in the Royal Navy of the eighteenth and nineteenth

The frigate *Unicorn*, Dundee docks.

centuries. An adventure playground to the right, modelled on the Battle of Camperdown, may have helped, but we didn't have time to dally. Conditions of service for the ratings were certainly poor, and this was the era of mutinies. Mutineers had struck on the *Bounty*, led by Fletcher Christian, against the unfortunate Captain Bligh in the Pacific Ocean in 1789. Admiral Duncan then experienced a major mutiny in virtually his entire North Sea Fleet in June 1797 as a protest against bad food, low pay and harsh treatment. The redoubtable admiral was still able to dupe his Dutch foes and hold them at anchor off Texel by sending signals between two British warships, the *Venerable* and *Adamant*. He was signalling the arrival of his fleet, which in reality was inactive and in a state of mutiny, and was determined that the Dutch would not pass through the narrow channel in which he was anchored. Duncan had learned of the shallow water in which he was anchored, and delighted in the knowledge that even if he was sunk, the British flag could still fly!

Such was the spirit of the imposing man of six-foot-four who led his fleet on 11th October into battle against the Dutch. Thousands of Dutch civilians watched the historic sea battle close to the Dutch coast which lasted a mere two and a half hours, but in which over 800 men were killed. Sixteen guns of the line faced each other in the time-honoured naval tradition, when Duncan deployed a new tactic and ordered his fleet to break the line and to engage an enemy ship of their own choosing to landward, in order to prevent the escape of the Dutch into shallow waters. The two Commanders-in-Chiefs faced each other, Admiral Duncan in his *Venerable* and Admiral de Winter in the *Vryheid*. 500 men were killed or wounded on these two ships alone. Duncan's chartacter rose to the occasion, and he shouted to his men: 'You see a severe Winter approaching. I have only to advise you to keep up a right good fire!'

He saved England from certain invasion by French troops by the destruction of the Dutch fleet, their proposed mode of transport, and returned a national hero. His action also signified the end of Holland as a major sea power, and led to the domination of the seas by the British. I passed the grandiose classical mansion with its nearby pinetum, once the home of this famous Dundonian. In our family another less famous Dundonian, is my wife, who was born a couple of miles down the road from Camperdown before her family moved to Bristol.

We survived a crossing of the golf course and the busy A923, the Coupar Angus road, and disappeared into the policies of Templeton Woods. The dog-walkers in the woods were strangely southern in appearance and habit, and one watched his spaniel swim in a pool, safe on the bank with a walkman and huge golfing brolly. Beyond the woodlands, tatty-roguers patrolled the furrows, alert as ever in the mist for diseased potatoes. I enjoyed the walk through the damp woodlands. It was the season of fungi — the yellows, browns and lilacs of the late summer woodland carpet. Ring doves, or *cushie doos*, voiced and echoed, and the atmosphere seemed damp and west coast rather than dry and Dundonian.

Beyond the division of Templeton and Clatto, signified by a water tower, we passed an old clump of bird cherries by a bend in the road. Siskins fed in the trees, and charms of goldfinches danced in the air. The countryside was a curious mixture of lanes and industry. The Milnes' house brought a smile to my lips! A bowling green appeared as an island of neatness in the midst of a smithy and a coup (rubbish tip) and an amazing shanty town of a plant hire enterprise where JCBs, cement mixers and tipper trucks surrounded a Portacabin office, with fresh washing hanging on the line beside them.

I began to climb the Sidlaws, which were invisible and covered in clart. As I splashed through the puddles of a rough track I spied several banknotes. Alas, they were foreign and printed 'test notes'. I examined the ground in some detail as I hauled up the steep, stony track. Eyebright flowers dotted the close-cropped

Mr and Mrs Milne,
Fallaws, Dundee.

sward. Linnets, curlews and a kestrel gave the walk an upland
feel once more. A motor-biker scrambled in silhouette up the
slope ahead and into the mists, reminding me that civilisation
was not far away. Before crossing the watershed of Balluderon
Hill, I turned south and peered through the murk. I should
have enjoyed a fine prospect over Dundee, the Tay, and Fife.
Instead I shrugged my shoulders and headed into the heather.
Only the bell heather was in flower. The ling, the real purple
heather of Andy Stewart fame, was still a week or two from

flowering. To the east stood one Scots pine, a lonely sentinel. I shook my head, and questioned how on earth this had survived the lightning, the sheep, and man?

We headed for a bleak block of pines in the glen below, and quickly lost height into Glen Ogilvie. There was trouble ahead. Meg had disturbed a wasps' byke in a bank by a gate, and we had to run for it. I discovered this angry scene halfway over the gate, with Meg pawing her muzzle, and my head surrounded by buzzing creatures. We broke all records for a descent into the steading of Nether Handwick, and although I had emerged unscathed — if breathless — Meg was a casualty of her own mischief and had been stung above the eye. Her eye troubled her for several miles. Oystercatchers on the dykes had black bills from feeding in the dark soil of the turnip fields; they were joined on the coping stanes by red-legged partridges. It was an enjoyable walk along the glen. Some way down I spotted a small dark mammal ahead on the roadside. It was fully occupied in its business, and as I approached it seemed completely oblivious to my presence. I ordered Meg to 'stay' and crept up on the water shrew, much bigger and darker than a common shrew. I knelt behind the creature, so close that I could hear it crunching the insect that it was eating. It had a very dark, almost black, glossy coat, and a tail as long as its body. It was a shrew alright, with a pointed snout. A minute or so passed. Small mammals don't usually get second chances, and I thought that perhaps this wee creature should be taught a lesson in self-defence, so I gently poked the animal's flank with a grass stalk. Its reaction was swift and dramatic! It squeaked loudly as it jumped in the air, and scampered into the roadside verge in an instant. Meg looked suitably anguished, missing out on the fun, with her running eye. It's a dog's life. I felt that I had done my bit for shrew training and conservation. Only the wings of the insect prey remained on the roadside as we headed north.

Another smiddy at Milton of Ogilvie sported the skilful creations of the blacksmith. The wall of the smithy was decorated with a horse's head and a peacock, both made of metal. There followed a trudge along the main road for a mile or so, then through the village of Charleston, a typical one-street Scottish village of one-storey cottages in various states of repair. Pampas grass and manicured lawns lined one roadside, whilst I preferred the stane dykes and white stonecrop on the other side.

More traditional still is the estate village of Glamis. Included in the neat village is the National Trust for Scotland's Angus Folk Museum which is a collection of seventeenth-century cottages. I bypassed the village centre and headed for Glamis Castle. It was Saturday and Glamis estate was closed, so I entered by a tradesman's entrance at the football pitch, and wandered up the main driveway through the *ha-ha* that kept the Highland cattle

*Grey Warrior*, Glamis.

and barley at bay. Glamis is impressive, the family home of the Earls of Strathmore and Kinghorne, and has been associated with royalty since the fourteenth century. Twentieth century connections are as impressive as the architecture, and the castle was the childhood home of Lady Elizabeth Bowes-Lyon, the wife of King George VI, better known to the nation as the Queen Mum. Princess Margaret was also born here.

We passed through the Glamis estate, by the doocot, and beneath the magnificent old oaks; then between the statues of James VI and his son Charles I, without meeting a soul; then up to the castle guarded by lions rampant; and we entered the estate woodlands and onto a disused railway line. Larger yellow, and the smaller white mulleins lined the trackside. We zig-zagged the back-lanes through the wet grass, and by means of wet legs and the Logie estate into Kirriemuir. Logie was a traditional estate, with pheasants everywhere, and complete with a tree-lined entrance drive, a coach house, big hoose, walled garden and lodges. It was a pleasant route into 'Kirrie' as the town is known locally. Kirrie was the birthplace of the novelist and playwright, Sir James M. Barrie. We descended the main road into the glen, past a small museum dedicated to the RAF, and overlooked the splendid mill buildings and a factory roofline which would have graced the Lancashire Pennine slopes. Kirrie is a winning blend of an old market-cum-industrial town, built on the braesides and based on water power, its tiers of terraces joined by tight closes. Recent decades have brought a weird and wonderful one-way system, fish and chip shops, and Italian ice-cream parlours.

One of the delights of the walk awaited us north of Kirrie, in the form of Caddam Wood, a lovely Scots pine woodland with a birch and beech under-storey, and a thick carpet of ripe blaeberries. Meg loves blaeberries, and so do I, and our passage through Caddam was suitably slow, as we revelled in the fruit and the woodland. Stinkhorns and other fungi, and the delightful cow-wheat flowers, completed my enjoyment. Sadly the wood then changed character into a dense spruce plantation. A standing stone to the north was a further disappointment, for it was an unimpressive structure at a list of 45°. *Three degrees* continued down more country lanes and through fresh rain and into the mists. The visibility north into the Angus glens was non-existent, and I was ending the day as it began, with a knowledge of views and little else.

We crossed a ford in spate, and passed hedgerows formed of an attractive mist of bluebells and lady's bedstraw. Suddenly we were atop Prosen bridge, and looking far down at Prosen Water with its black peaty pools, the haunt of salmon and subject of folklore. We had made Glen Prosen, and though I couldn't see them, I knew that high hills lay ahead.

# Part VII   The Scottish Highlands

## Glen Clova to Ballater

As logistics would have it, we travelled a nine-mile stretch of Glen Clova by car, and by way of Cortachy and Dykehead we assumed the next day's starting point on the east bank of the Esk at Wheen. The southern entrance of Glen Clova has two guards: the Airlie Memorial Tower perched high on Tulloch Hill, and an awful piece of castlellated architecture in the form of a hostelry at Dykehead. Persevere beyond Dykehead, and Glen Clova is among the loveliest of glens, classically formed by ice and water, and striped by heather swathes and plantations in its lower reaches, with lofty crags, lochans and forests to the north. These Angus glens are a well-kept secret, known mostly to fishermen, stalkers and hill-walkers.

Once again the weather was poor. It was raining and the river South Esk was as still as a millpond. A heron stood sentinel, and a short-eared owl wove a capricious hunter's web through the air. Its pallid form, alert face and elegant wings lent an air of hope to the greyness ahead. Glen Clova is well farmed, and has a clutter of stock — sheep, cattle and even a herd of goats. The hillsides moved with rabbits, and Meg became dizzy with

Grouse whirred away
on anxious wings
— *Glen Clova.*

Airplane wreckage,
Muckle Cairn, Angus.

excitement. Beehives lined the roadside: the bees had been transported into the glen to harvest the nectar from the heather. An upland jumble of peewits, wheatears and curlews called, yet despite their efforts a peaceful atmosphere presided over the glen. I climbed from the steading on a track upwards to Loch Wharral, aiming for a plantation edge. Grouse whirred away on anxious wings and crackled their staccato calls at us. Only a few days' peace remained for the red grouse, for it was almost the *glorious twelfth,* when the glens of the north-east would resound to the retorts of shotguns, and the grouse would be dead and braced. A little higher still, and Dreish and Mayar, the mountains to the north of Clova, commanded the glen. They are strange hills, with apparently uninteresting plateaux for their summits, but they have spectacular crag-lines to the north and east, too rotten for climbing, but the home of alpine flowers and falcons.

Heavy weather rumbled in from the south. Grouse butts began to appear on each horizon. A pair of ravens *kronked* over, followed by a youngster with a strange falsetto voice. Suddenly Loch Wharral was in view, surrounded by crags in a hanging corrie. I stopped to enjoy this majesty, but the weather was catching up, so we scurried onto the peaty upland plateau, haunt of dozens of blue mountain hares. The weather had us after all, and the mists closed in. Navigation along plateaux in mist isn't easy, and I had to use the lochans and relief to steer us over Muckle Cairn. A snipe lifted noisily out of a burn and one lochan held two lesser black-backed gulls. In fact the walking was pleasant through poorly developed peat hags, across the short turf and blaeberry of the undulating plateau. South-east of the summit I made a detour to investigate the wreckage of an aircraft. Somehow the patter of the rain on the twisted lattice gave an eerie quality to the scene. A tail section and two engines provided evidence of an air-crash, otherwise it was a hopeless tangle of despair and scorched earth. We hurried away.

On the descent from Muckle Cairn we encountered a large herd of around seventy red deer hinds. Grouse continued to explode away from us with monotonous regularity, and the sweet calls of half-a-dozen plovers provided a hillside flecked with gold. Cairns were flecked with quartz. We negotiated a more difficult area of entrenched peat hags, and I cursed the route and my wet feet. Loch Lee appeared out of the mist, far below, and in no time at all we had gained a Landrover track which would speed us off the hill and towards Glen Lee. Mount Keen's cone loomed ahead, two ridges away, through a monotone of greyness which culminated in the lightness of Loch Lee itself. A fishing boat on the loch helped to give a sense of scale. It began to rain hard, but this was a lovely stretch of the walk. Below me were the spectacular wooded crags of Carlochy, before Glen Lee swept eastward in glacial symmetry.

As we passed through the mature larch plantation of Inchgrundle, I spied a keeper dressing rabbits at the burn. Keepers are fickle creatures, and should be played carefully, especially if you're travelling with a dog. Naturally enough, their approachability usually varies with the season, and they tend to be over-cautious if not downright suspicious of walkers' intentions in the stalking period. We were out of season, just, and this boy was happy to talk, and he told me a lot about the

Keeper skinning
rabbits, Inchgrundle,
Glen Lee.

area. He kept one of a half-dozen beats of the Dalhousie estate,
and was of lithe build, with a fresh face. A prominent gold filling
flashed through the rain and his conversation. He spoke of a
busy year, occupied with grouse, deer, salmon and estate tasks,
as well as working with many continental clients ('those with the
money — Germans and Dutch mostly'). All the time we talked,
he continued his task of skinning and gutting the rabbits. He
made it look easy. One cut across the shoulder blades was all that
was required in order to peel the whole skin off. The intestines

153

and lower guts were removed, but the organs were left inside. His quarry had been shot at night with an airgun, and were all youngsters — the flesh on the older rabbits was too tough, and they were much more difficult to skin. When I questioned him about the preponderance of hares on the hill, he answered in terms of an annual bag of 'several thousand'. An aircraft droned overhead and I was reminded of the wreck on the hillside. I asked if he remembered any accidents. He knew only of a Lancaster bomber which had come down in the war, but remembered a horrifying crash involving a modern jet fighter which ploughed into a hillside only a mile and a half from his previous home in Wigtownshire. With a countryman's air, he went on to say that the big bang and the shaking of his house weren't as bad as the blue flashing lights and heavy security which followed. We parted and he wished me well.

During our conversation he had learned of my intentions, my route and my dog. I wandered away thinking well of the estate. His information was supplemented by a sign by the river, headed 'East Grampian Deer Management Group'. The sign requested the co-operation of visitors and explained why and when the deer needed to be controlled, and how the visitors could assist, primarily by keeping to preferred routes and by keeping dogs on leads. Since the last wolf was killed in Scotland in the early eighteenth century, red deer have had no natural predators, save man, and if left uncontrolled they multiply rapidly, leading to starvation and disease. They therefore need to be controlled. Stalking red deer makes a significant contribution to the economy of the Highlands of Scotland through the income generated by stalkers and their needs. On the negative side, deer forests and estates (with the earlier and more notorious introduction of sheep) have been responsible for population clearances and the continued loss of native forests. Young trees can't withstand incessant grazing, so much of Scotland's native forest stock is ageing and doomed. Most of our 'deer forests' are bare expanses of open hill, and far from being true forest animals, Scottish red deer have adapted to these harsher conditions. They are much smaller than their English woodland cousins. In fact, Scottish deer farmers cross hinds gathered from the hill with large southern parkland stags.

Along the shore of Loch Lee the rain began to ease. The dark glassy water collected the raindrops. It provided a mirror for the trout to disturb, and was skimmed by house martins, their backs the colour of the water itself, so that only a myriad of white rumps danced along the surface. A ruined kirk on the east shore surrounded by ancient ash trees was a superb setting for the sun to break free of the rainclouds. Gravestones in the kirkyard, mementos of more populous times, were lit once again by the sun, which warmed the final resting places of Donald

Donald McDonel's gravestone, Kirkton, Glen Lee.

McDonel (1733) and Alexander Ross (1784), the latter the author of poems in the Scottish dialect. The oldest stone I could find was dated 1696, with a Latin inscription. Invermark holds a cluster of estate houses in addition to the lodge itself, a splendid piece of Victoriana — all stone, spires and turrets. It is surrounded by a high hedge over which two giant redwoods loom, and nestles in a birchwood with delicious scents after the rain. Above the boiling mists of Glen Esk to the east stood the ruin of Invermark Castle and a strange conical monument set

A monument to the Forest of Caledon? Hill of Rowan, Glen Esk.

high on the Hill of Rowan.

We turned north again and passed two deer targets in the birch woods. Stalkers are always tested by the keepers before being granted a shot at their live quarry. Shortly afterwards another keeper drove by in a Landrover, one hand on the wheel and one using a radio. Stalking has come a long way from its early days, and those of us who love the hills wish that modern clients would emulate their Victorian predecessors and spend their days walking to their sport on the well-engineered stalkers' paths. Instead we have Landrover tracks bulldozed into the hills, all in the name of comfort and ease. Along the Water of Mark is another quintessential piece of Victoriana, the Queen's Well. Shaped in the form of a crown, the Well's pedigree is explained by a plaque which reads:

> Her Majesty Queen Victoria and His Royal Highness the Prince Consort visited this well and drank of its refreshing waters on 20th September 1861, the year of Her Majesty's great sorrow.

Queen Victoria was a great lover of the Highlands, and many a panorama can boast of being the 'Queen's View'. Her interest in Scotland began the fashion of acquiring Highland estates and

The Queen's Well,
Glen Mark.

wearing tartan. It seems that the Highlands have been owned by
tartan-clad absentee landlords ever since.

Rain fell heavily again as we began the climb onto Mount
Keen, by the cottage of Glen Mark. The cottage porch revealed
what life in Glenmark is all about. Here lay a storm-lamp and
oilskins, fishing rods and Calor gas bottles. Sheep sheltered
under a bench outside the cottage. Three hikers coming off the
hill passed us, and spoke of 'no views and much rain'. Sure
enough, we arrived on the summit of Mount Keen at 3,077 feet

(939 metres) amidst blocks of pink wet granite. It wasn't possible to see down into Glen Tanar. I dallied and was rewarded by the rain stopping. Silence descended. I left the summit reluctantly, my 226th Munro, and marvelled at the displays of light to the west. Squalls and shafts of light highlighted the spectacular corrie of Lochnagar to the west, and the tors of Ben Avon in the Cairngorms to the north-west. To a hill man, such experiences are life-giving. Scottish Rights of Way Society signs brought me back to reality, and I moved speedily over the Mounth Road, by the Shiel of Glentanar and over the ridge down towards Ballater. Climbing out of Glen Tanar, I began to tire and rifled my pockets for glucose tablets. Emotionally I was fed by a rainbow over the Caledonian pinewoods of Tanar and over the hilltop, Glen Muick and Lochnager raised my spirits. I sat in the breeze above Glen Muick absorbing the atmosphere as four red deer hinds made off. A pair of buzzards hunted overhead, and I was a mere speck in the midst of some turbulence and dramatic light. There were many special moments during my *three degrees* quest, sometimes provided by the landscapes, sometimes by the wildlife, and sometimes by the people.

Above the birchwoods of Glen Muick that August evening I felt that my walk had been vindicated, and I descended into the plantations a contented man. By the Bridge of Muick I expanded my lungs to the sweet scent of lime flowers and renewed my acquaintance with Queen Victoria. Here it was, in the familiar territory of her Balmoral estate, that she met the 1st Battalion of the Gordon Highlanders on 16th September 1899, prior to their embarkation for the Boer War. Ballater was all bunting across the streets, a nod of recognition from the age of Elizabeth to that of Victoria. I thought of Innerleithen.

# 27 Grouse Muirs

## Ballater to River Deveron

Ballater was busy and oozed festival Victoriana. Women in shawls and gentlemen in black suits accompanied the bunting. Out of town on the Deeside fields, marquees also hinted at festivity but I hadn't time to linger, for a long walk beckoned over high ground, and I was anxious to be underway. Despite the festivities, the farmers were busy turning hay on this fine August day. Near the cemetery at Milton of Tullich we turned northward and into the Crannach.

I had tentatively arranged to meet some friends in the woodland here, and no sooner had we entered the birch wood than we were greeted by Rick and Elizabeth striding through the bushy ling and blaeberries. Accompanying them was somebody I was keen to talk with, Robin Callander, part-owner of the woodland, and a man with ideas. Rick and Elizabeth had camped in the wood overnight. Rick's a forester, and a zany one at that, who lives, eats and breathes trees. ('There's no better way to experience a woodland than to sleep in it!') Elizabeth is an American and simply enjoys Scotland. I can think of worse ways to enjoy Scotland than accompanied by Rick's zest and enthusiasm. I had heard of Robin through Rick and rangering circles, for listed amongst his talents is his prowess as a drystane dyker — by appointment to Her Majesty the Queen, no less — and he is often called upon to pass on his skills to rangers. Today, though, I wanted to talk to him about the Crannach.

Robin and three colleagues have recently bought the Crannach from Captain Farquarson, the owner of Invercauld estate. They plan to re-establish and guarantee the survival of its native Scottish woodland. It is an attractive site since, of the 500 hectares, one-third is already established with a glorious birch, juniper and Scots pine woodland. Moreover, the heathland on the hill and beneath the trees is unusually rich in herbs with an important bearberry community. Bearberry is a rather less common member of the *Erica* family, with small white or pinkish flowers which form bright red berries. Robin's plans for the Crannach are to manage the block of established woodland, to replant another third and to leave one-third as open hill. Deer control is seen as essential to the success of the trees. Already he wished to emulate the well-organised East Grampian Deer Management Group, and is optimistic about getting support from other estates. At present they're only culling five stags a year from the hill, which is insufficient for the long-term

Robin Callander in his birchwoods.

conservation of the forest. He assured me that some of the Scots pines on his western march, by the Tullich burn, were objects of tremendous character, and of great importance to the gene pool of Scottish forestry. Robin is a learned and influential figure, and I wished him well with his plans. As we continued along the track, redpolls trilled overhead, a golden ringed dragonfly patrolled our route and a burst of purple greeted us as we emerged onto the open hill. The ling was in flower. A combination of smells of birch and heather, the specks of rain

Deer in window,
Hillockhead,
Grampian.

and the colours, prompted the thought that this indeed was Scotland — *Caledonia* of old.

White flags fluttered in the purple heather. These were Rick's *tatter flags,* set on the hillside to establish the wind speeds and site-exposure. Quite literally the flags tatter, and the rate at which they do so indicates the suitability of the terrain for planting trees. Robin had already planted 30,000 trees in three years, but was planting still: he wanted to know to what height he could go.

As we ascended the weather began to clear. Ahead lay the massive lump of Morvern, whilst behind us Mount Keen's cone peeked above Deeside. Morvern presented a problem, a classic orienteer's dilemma — should I go the short way and climb it, or take a longer course and skirt it? My decision was a good old British compromise, and I skirted around its south-west flank and over the western *bealach*. This was a wise decision for it took us through an area of prostrate juniper, with magnificent views south-west to Lochnagar. A hard, hard pull up to the saddle enabled me to savour the scents and sounds of Morvern — grasshoppers, thyme, eyebright and harebells. On the high ground the community changed to one of cloudberry, and the turf was interspersed with its large raspberry-like fruits, a sign of the advancing season. The cloudberry leaves were already exhibiting shades of deep red and purple.

We followed a burn down the north flank of Morvern, and plunged into the Tornashean forest for what turned out to be a frustrating thrash around forest rides and non-existent footpaths. Each long walk has its nadir — and this was it. Our entrance to the forest had seemed promising enough. There was a hint of birdlife at the forest edge, with wrens, goldcrests and ring doves. As I worried about how to get Meg across the deer fence, a roe deer bounded away ahead of us, and bolted underneath the fence — perfect! Nemesis followed, however, and in no time at all the faint path had expired and we jinked along forest rides in an intuitive search for an exit. It was rarely possible to see beyond the wall of trees, and I had no compass to

Salmon, River Don.

confirm our direction. I could use the position of the sun or the relief of the land, and for some time I searched in vain for a line of pylons which crossed the forest and were the key to our escape. Eventually I found release, but not before calling the whole project and my sanity into question. Once clear of the forest, I discovered a couple of Grampian characters who restored my inner calm. The first was the farmer at Hillockhead, who complained about the weather and delivered a series of musical 'ayes'. Shortly afterwards I spoke with the local mobile grocer, and he told me with some pride that he had been doing the same round for fifty-seven years, starting in 1931 with a horse and cart. He had worn out four vans in the process. In the same lilting accent he said: 'I'm up here every Saturday. I sometimes miss awhiles in the winter on account of the sna'.'

Tornashean hadn't finished with us yet, though, and we crossed another spur of the forest on our northward route. This time we were on a well-defined, if wet, track, and all went well. Jays screeched within the forest. At the forest edge was a herb nursery, a useful enterprise, but not to the long-distance walker. For two or three miles we followed the course of the main road, the A97, but it wasn't busy, and afforded pleasant walking, during which I was able to admire several species of fungi, including some parasol mushrooms. Rows of silage bags and Tilhill forestry plantations also diverted my attention from the tarmac — riveting stuff, I know, but walking along roads is like that!

At Bridge of Buchat a roadside worthy picking raspberries stopped me for a chat. He had a bucket tied around his waist with a piece of old rope. Once he knew my route, his conversation became excited and he related memories of his

Meg and raspberry
picker, Bridge of
Buchat.

crossings of the hills in his youth, speaking of the *roadies* (tracks)
and 'the old way by the red ford'. He told me of an unfortunate
chap heading for the Cabrach who had holed his boot and died
of poison in the wound. He reckoned that I'd be over (to the
Cabrach) in an hour. I reckoned that he must have been a bit of
a greyhound in his younger days. True, he was slight and wiry,
and as he pulled at his pipe I left him to his rasps.

Glenbuchat Castle,
Grampian.

A farmer at Easter Buchat told me the best route over the hills to the Cabrach. 'Cabrach' is on the map. *The Cabraich* it is in the lilting, singing dialect, never far from the Welsh. We took the track past Blackhillock and Drumnagarrow, climbed Meikle Firbriggs, and looked back in astonishment at Glenbuchat and the Don. It was early evening, and the lengthening day produced some stunning light. Glenbuchat Castle was centre-stage, a sixteenth-century Gordon castle, whose last laird joined the '45 at the tender age of 68 years. He escaped Culloden and subsequently Scotland, as a rebel. Above his castle entrance remains the inscription: 'Nothing on earth remains bot fame'.

A joyous walk on an easy track followed, over the tops towards the Cabrach. We disturbed a roe at close quarters. Her coat was on fire, in the light of the gloamin'. Profiles of mountain hares and roe deer crossed the horizon. Scotland was beautiful on that evening as we entered the silence of the hills. Beyond Creag an Eun the peat took over, and a bog stomp ensued across to Sand hill. Small but spectacular crags were of interest on Creag an Sgor to the south-west, but the dominant feature was a hill shrouded in mist to the north-east, the Buck. As if to emphasise the name, four red deer moved across the hillside. I could now see my objective of *The Cabraich* in the distance, and my stride quickened. Grouse muirs and spent cartridges were all around us, and the landscape was striated with the patterns of the managed heather. At a burn I gulped down a half-litre of water before running away from the midges. The light was fading and I needed to hurry. A big fat toad lumbered along our track. Here are the headwaters of the River Deveron, and in the ailing light by Powneed, a dipper and a heron disappeared into the gloom along the youthful river.

Ah, the welcome sight of the yellow lights of the shooting lodge at Cabrach! I had been walking for ten hours and was in need of some rest. A deer farm and some Highland cattle proved more interesting still in the gloom, full of strange noises and shapes. Kate should have been waiting for me at the post office but wasn't. I didn't have the energy to question why, and simply made ready to fall asleep leaning against my rucksack. Before I could do so, an employee of the hunting lodge offered to drive me around the loop of a minor road in what turned out to be a fruitless search for her. He told me that he was from Devon, and had fancied a change. Some change! As he was returning me to the post office, we passed Kate and I thanked my good Samaritan. Our car's exhaust had been troublesome, hence the delay. We camped off the Rhynie road in a field full of sleep.

# 28 The Speyside Way

## Dufftown to Spey Bay

We had camped overnight in the middle of nowhere, along with Kate's sister and nephews up from Norfolk, with their French pen-friend, an ambassador for the Auld Alliance. My nephews were keen to join in on this wayward quest of a mad uncle, and we spent the day walking the Speyside Way from Dufftown to Spey Bay. And so we drove along the A941, past the Cabrach and into Dufftown. Readers with a predilection for the amber fluid, the water of life (*uisgebeatha* in the Gaelic), will know of Dufftown and the Fiddich. Speyside is a major centre of Scotch malt whisky production, and of Dufftown in particular it has been said that:

> Rome was built on seven hills,
> Dufftown on its seven stills.

The town predates the Act of Parliament in 1823 which was passed to help rationalise and tax whisky production in licensed distilleries (rather than in illegal stills). It was founded in 1817 by James Duff, the 4th Earl of Fife, and has the wide streets and gridiron pattern of a planned town. A settlement had been present nearby since the thirteenth century, on the site of Balvenie Castle, one of the largest castles in the north at the time. Many Scottish kings in the early medieval period chose to rule from the north-east, for it was well provided with castles. Balvenie was important, and so was visited by such names from history as Edward I of England, and the Wolf of Badenoch, Alexander Stewart, prince of the realm and brother to Robert III. The Wolf held tyrannical sway over the north-east in the thirteenth century.

Dufftown was also bedecked with bunting, just as Innerleithen and Ballater had been, and once more I wondered what I'd done to deserve the welcome. We turned north at the clock tower, and took the Speyside Way just by the Glenfiddich distillery. The town still has its seven distilleries, and boasts the oldest in Scotland, the Mortlach distillery which was founded in the same year as the Whisky Act of 1823. Glenfiddich is a famous distillery, founded by Major William Grant and, aptly, his seven sons. Whisky was first distilled there on Christmas Day 1887. Thousands of tourists now visit its whisky centre each year, but it was early on Sunday morning and the centre was closed. We set off along the disused railway track which forms an extension to

Glenfiddich Distillery,
Dufftown.

the long-distance route, a south-east spur from Craigellachie to
Dufftown.

Walking along disused railways is easy but generally
disappointing, since they're invariably hemmed in by hedgerows
or cuttings. We were treated to occasional views of the Fiddich
racing below, but for the most part had to content ourselves with
the parochial horizons of our line ahead. Evidence of the
limestone geology of these parts was provided by the tall and
delightful nettle-leaved bellflowers, a treat I'm more accustomed
to in the limestone woods of Shropshire! Limestone outcrops are
rare in Scotland. Scotch Argus butterflies were plentiful along
the dappled tracksides, and buzzards mewed and circled
overhead. Kininvie, a sixteenth-century tower-house, gleamed
white in the sun, its baronial turrets and crow-stepped gables
resplendent in the August sunshine. Our pace and progress
were good as we covered the four miles to Craigellachie in
pursuit of the Auld Alliance with Bertrand, in a flurry of
*Franglais*.

Craigellachie is another distillery settlement, and the silvery
chimneys glittered above the dark green softwoods of the gorge.
Telford, that ubiquitous civil engineer, arrived here in 1815, and
built a splendid iron bridge across the Spey. This eastern
Craigellachie (there is another at Aviemore in Inverness-shire
forty miles to the south-east) is reputed to represent the eastern-
most domain of Clan Grant, and their slogan is 'Stand Fast,
Craigellachie'. We passed the Fiddichside Inn, with its collection
of old enamel signs — *McEwans*, *Whitbread* and *Bristol Tipped
Cigarettes* — and were rewarded with our first view of the Spey.

The Spey may be named after the Gaelic *speidh* meaning rapidity, and is Scotland's fastest-flowing river, famous for salmon, timber and floods. It drains over 1,300 square miles of mountainous terrain, and flows ninety-eight miles to the sea at Spey Bay. Its waters are capable of rising swiftly, and in the great flood of August 1829 the river rose almost six metres and left an unparalleled scene of destruction of property and crops. Three thousand Highlanders were left destitute. We kept the river on our left as we passed through the cool woodlands and the manicured lawns of Arndilly House. Soon we were climbing the flank of Ben Aigan, in the Forestry Commission's property of Craigellachie, still with the Speyside Way. Once again our horizons were limited by trees, and the Speyside Way was a disappointment. Its route was rarely on the riverside, sometimes even on roads, and our outlook was frequently limited to the road or car ahead. Just as we were beginning to despair of the forest, a wonderful vista opened up: a view northward into the Moray Firth, and a foreground with the classic profile of a river making its final way out to sea between dark forests. Shortly afterwards we met two long-distance walkers sweltering their Way. They were loaded up to the hilt and surrounded by flies. We felt guilty about our lightweight approach to the day as we ran down the hillside and along the forest edge to lunch at Boat o' Brig.

The name Boat o' Brig — boat of the bridge — tells a curious tale. An ancient and important wooden bridge, perhaps the first to cross the Spey, was washed away and replaced by a ferryboat. The bridge was not rebuilt until the present one was erected in the early nineteenth century. We took lunch beneath the railway, to the constant barking of the bouncing black labradors and the brown and white spaniels of nearby kennels. Meg ignored the tumult and concentrated instead on our sandwiches. Next came a dull five-mile stretch along a road adjacent to the Forestry Commission woodlands. It was Sunday afternoon and the drivers were out. Fochaber's skyline of church spire and Milne High School came gradually closer. At last the path turned off the road and followed a burn, its banks carpeted with tall lilac valerian flowers. Fochabers is famous for its tree nurseries and we walked first along fields full of young *leylandii* and spruce, then between the mature *leylandii* of suburban gardens. Suburban Fochabers was alarmingly similar to suburban *Anywhere,* and consisted of allotments and gardens full of pink sunburned bodies. At last the route met the Spey at a park to the west of Fochabers town centre. Fochabers is another of the planned towns of the northern Spey Valley, and was created on its present site in the late eighteenth century when Gordon Castle (a mile to the north of the town) was rebuilt. This historic estate has been the home over the centuries of the Earls and

Stone salmon, 1630,
Tugnet.

Marquises of Huntly, who in turn became the Dukes of Gordon.
Much of the estate was sold to the Crown in 1935, which enabled
the Forestry Commission to plant the large Forest of Fochabers
which had been prominent from Ben Aigan.

Richard called a halt at the park to appraise the standard of
cricket. He was unimpressed by the multi-coloured attire of the
teams, and by the fieldsmen who smoked. The wicketkeeper
used the opportunity to sunbathe and wore shorts and pads
only. I reminded Richard that Scottish cricket was not
completely devoid of talent, and cited Freuchie in Fife (page
136). The ground had a pleasant setting, with Fochabers church
spire as a backdrop.

Beyond the crazy golf course lay the two bridges of Fochabers,
the old brig which had been swept away in the Great Flood of
1829 and rebuilt, and the modern bridge of 1972. Across the
Spey lay the Baxter's food factories of Mosstodloch. Another
mile along a busy B-road followed. Whoever planned the
Speyside Way's route needs his head examining — long-distance
walkers and motorcars don't mix. Kate had joined us for the
final five miles, and we marched along the road anxious to be rid
of the traffic. We preferred the black waters of the fast-flowing
Spey.

*No Camping, No Caravans, No Canoeing.* Notices abounded. No
anything. We sped through the forests and the fields, full of
combine dust and smells. The oilseed rape was being harvested,
and the speckled wood and small tortoiseshell butterflies were on
the wing. I felt cheated and annoyed with myself at being lured
along a long-distance route when other alternatives had been
forsaken. But as often happens, the reward came at the end of
the day when we passed the old viaduct of the former coastal

Flat-bottomed salmon
boats, Tugnet.

railway from Elgin to Aberdeen and walked the last mile of the
Spey to Tugnet. It was only at Tugnet that the Spey became
alive, and its history and power obvious. It seemed that the long-
distance route had kept us away from the river, and at Tugnet,
at last, it greeted us. An old ice-house dated 1630, and a
collection of eighteenth-century buildings, vividly reminded us
of the importance of salmon fishing.

Salmon boxes are enormous, much bigger than the usual fish
boxes of the Scottish pelagic fleets. They were piled against the
buildings, and against the strangely designed boats which have
special flat bottoms to cope with the shallow river. Nets were
drying in the sun, and a shingle bank hid from view the crashing
waves of the Moray Firth. This bank is created by long-shore
drift, which diverts the treacherous river towards the village of
Kingston on the west bank. Periodic cuts are made through the
bank in order to free the Spey and reduce the risk of flooding.

Kingston-on-Spey was named after its Yorkshire namesake by
the Yorkshiremen who founded its shipbuilding yard in 1786,
lured north by the availability of Speyside timber. Its yards built
many famous ships, the tea clippers and 'Cape Horners' of the
eighteenth and nineteenth centuries. Timber from the great
Speyside forests of Abernethy, Glenmore and those of the Duke
of Gordon was floated downriver in times of spate. 'Floating'
began in earnest after the York Buildings Company commenced
activity in 1719. The statistics are mind-boggling — 60,000 trees
bought off Grant at Abernethy alone in 1728, resulting in
thousands of trees going downriver to Speymouth for export to
England.

Abernethy Forest and
Cairngorms, remnant
Caledonian pine.

Abernethy and Rothiemurchus forests consist of old
gnarled trees today, simply because their fine ancestors were cut
out by the York Buildings Company and others. Rocks were
removed from the Spey to facilitate floatings — large fires were
lit under rocks when the water level was low, and water was
thrown over the hot rocks to fracture them for removal. Teams
of floaters presided over the timber journeys either from the
banks, using long poles, or from rafts on the water. Even *curachs*
(coracles) made of leather and wood were used, and a famous
Speyside worthy named *Alastair Mor na Curach* (big Alastair of
the coracle) lived to the ripe old age of 106! Not all his
colleagues were so lucky — floating was a dangerous game and
many were crushed or drowned in the river, or lost at sea.
Floaters were idle for much of the year, since their trade could
only be conducted in times of spate, yet they always managed to
pay the rents for their crofts out of their floating dues.

I scrambled up the shingle bank to seek out the Moray Firth
and my northward line. It was hazy and impossible to see far. I
sympathised with the floaters, drifting out to sea in a *haar*, never
to be seen again.

# Part VIII  The Far North

# 29

# The Caithness Coast

## Wick to John o' Groats

*'The Lowlands beyond the Highlands'*

Wick's Norse origins are as basic as its name, which is Norse for bay or inlet. On a September morning the harbour was bright and breezy, and full of fishing boats. The ice factory, fuel tankers, lifeboat and cranes had a restful Sunday morning air about them. Our objective was to walk along the coast from Papigoe and Staxigoe villages, north to Noss Head and the castles of Girnigoe and Sinclair. Wick's old core is to the north of the river, with a planned new town of artisan dwellings to the south. The new town was built quickly and poorly, to accommodate the population boom of the early nineteenth century, based on the herring fishing. Wick's fortunes have followed the fishing, and with the collapse of the herring the town has had to diversify. So the famous Caithness Glass Company is now to be found here, although a small fishing fleet still remains.

The landscapes of Caithness are influenced by the low-lying ancient rocks of the Devonian age, the old red sandstones. These sedimentary rocks were laid down 370 million years ago in a vast freshwater basin named *Lake Orcadie*. Intervening dry spells have resulted in a rock which splits easily along laminations. Caithness flagstones have been shipped commercially throughout Britain since the end of the eighteenth century, and the northern towns of Wick, Thurso and Kirkwall have relied heavily on the trade. So too have builders and dykers, and it is not unusual to see cottage roofs made of flags, and fields fenced with them. Indeed, the Caithness Flagstone Quarrying Company shipped its products worldwide and in 1877 proudly proclaimed that 'after a trial of . . . the principal towns in England, Scotland, Ireland, the Colonies and South America, it has proved itself to be one of the best paving stones known'. It was an industry unique to this area and was known as the pavement trade. Output peaked at the turn of the century with 35,000 tons per annum, but its fortunes were to crash even before the Great War, and many of its workers emigrated to Canada. A remnant of the industry still survives, producing top-quality stones for specialist markets.

The dykes of Staxigoe were certainly made of flags. Its small harbour has a curious rock pinnacle which presides over the small boats. Out to sea a supertanker appeared as large as the island it was passing, the Skerries, easily recognisable by its twin

Fish lorry, Wick.

lights. It is the only lighthouse in Britain with two towers, and the second oldest in the nation, dating from 1794. Staxigoe was a hive of industry or play. Kids with bikes whizzed everywhere, and a small boy yelled excitedly 'the barley's on!' The farmers were indeed busy harvesting the barley, and tractors attended the combine like workers around a queen bee. It was exhilarating to be along a cliff line again, for not since Lyme Regis and Weston had we experienced this type of terrain. Bedding planes in the cliffs caught the sunlight and seemed to be stacked like layers of paper from the sea. Lichen the colour of paprika covered the rocks, and mushrooms grew in the short turf of the cliffs. They were delicious, we ate them for supper! Grey seals, shags and great black-backs cavorted offshore, along with a raft of eider. It was sunny and fresh and great to be alive.

Fulmars hung
motionless in the
breeze
    *— Caithness.*

Towards Noss Head we discovered an awesome abyss, with rock doves and sea asters inside. Far below came the gurgling and sucking noises of a primitive force. There are caves all along the coastline. About the caves are the bedding planes, and about the bedding planes, seabirds, lichens and flowers. By Noss Head light we admired the flying skills of the fulmars and rock doves as they hung motionless in the breeze. *A bonxie* or great skua, a predatory gull-like bird, came along and scattered the source of our pleasure.

A mile west of Noss Head lie the twin castles of Girnigoe and Sinclair, historic seat of the Earls of Caithness. Girnigoe is a fifteenth-century castle, and the most important and impressively situated on a narrow neck of rock on a mini-peninsula. We explored Girnigoe and found two passages, one

Castles Girnigoe and Sinclair, Caithness.

to a dungeon, and the other which led down some steps to the sea. Castle Sinclair is the seventeenth-century wing to the west of Girnigoe, although both castles are now badly ruined. Rain was threatening and so we thumbed a lift back south to the car from a London couple, who had recently retired to Papigoe. He liked it but she didn't, which seemed like a recipe for disaster rather than a long and happy retirement.

We motored north around Sinclair's Bay, and resumed *three degrees* at Skirza, around three miles south of Duncansby Head, along from John o' Groats. *Three degrees* is in fact just offshore of Caithness, but I was well inside my self-imposed 'five minute' rule — the amount of leeway which I was usually prepared to stray. My route kissed the coast and the clifftops, and that was fine by me. Skirza could only have been in Scotland. Peats were stacked outside the cottages, and a silo lay stricken on its side. We resumed the route at a small quarry which perhaps had won the flags in a more prosperous period. Spectacular cliffs up to seventy metres in height lay between Duncansby Head and Skirza. *Bonxies* patrolled the clifftops, gannets patrolled the waters offshore, and seals pointed their snouts skyward. A roe

The Pyramids of the North, Duncansby Stacks.

deer with two kids bounded away from the edge, conspicuous without tree cover.

With excitement rising I realised that I could now see water on three sides of the headland, and we were nearing the end of *third degree* mainland. Closer still came the celebrated stacks of Duncansby, the fishing boats off the headland, the Orkneys and the squalls overhead. Perhaps the finest natural features of the whole walk were immediately before us — the five stacks of Duncansby. Two of the pointed stacks are as high as, if not higher than, the nearby cliffs. Muckle (big) Stack is ninety-nine metres high whilst its neighbour Little Stack is seventy-three metres, but their drama results from the combination of height, shape and position. They are the pyramids of the north, set in the deep turbulent waters of the Pentland Firth, famed for its tidal rips. Muckle Stack in fact has twin peaks, and a pair of ravens played in its eddies. It was a beautiful and a haunting spot, epitomised by the baying of the seals on the rocks offshore. Their wailing resounded around the canyons of the coast, rising above the crash of the waves and the pulls of the wind. We found a dead short-eared owl on the clifftop which exhibited the classic signs of a peregrine kill — a scattering of feathers around a plucked and eaten breast. Raptor had killed raptor in the constant struggle for survival. As if to confirm our suspicions, a peregrine hurried across the wind, all dark and menacing, more so even than the *bonxies*.

Duncansby Head light is short and squat. There is no need for height since it is perched atop the cliffs. A massive foghorn complements the light. Offshore the wild waters of the Pentland Firth pour back and forth between the Atlantic Ocean and the North Sea at a rate of up to twelve knots. In the days of sail, ships could find it impossible to pass through the Firth against the currents which are the fastest in Britain, and among the fastest in the world. Tidal rips called *The Bores* and *The Merry Men of Mey* are avoided by mariners, as is the largest whirlpool off the British coast, *The Swilkie of Stroma*. Norse and Scots folklore attribute the whirlpool to a sunken miller's wheel which continually grinds salt beneath the waters.

A couple of miles to the west of Duncansby Head is the small but infamous village of John o' Groats. It is entirely given over to tourism, with souvenir shops and an information centre which capitalise on its appeal as 'the last place'. Somehow it appeared almost seedy, though not long after we visited the roof of mainland Britain it was sold to a developer who intends to revitalise the site. By the hotel and the pier for the passenger ferry to Orkney lies the 'Last House in Scotland'. John o' Groats is named after a fifteenth-century Dutchman, John de Groot. He was the ferryman to Orkney and charged fourpence a trip, hence the 'groat'. In the fifteenth century Orkney had come under Scottish control, from Norway, and James IV was anxious to secure a ferry link in order to assimilate the islands into the realm. De Groot made a success of his enterprise, and in time his family began to quarrel over who should succeed him in his old age. In order to still their quarrels he built an eight-sided house, with eight doors and an eight-sided table. In this way no one could be looked upon as the head of the household.

John o' Groats is 876 miles from Land's End, and almost 600 miles from Lyme Regis on my *three degrees* course. The full, marathon route was apparently first tackled by an American, Buritt, in 1865, a journey which took him several months. Super-fit walkers can now do it in around ten days, and athletes can cycle it in less than two! Our walk through mainland Britain had taken the best part of a month, though we rarely rushed, and, quite the converse, frequently stopped to savour our surroundings. Despite the glare of tourism it was an appropriate halt to the mainland line, and a teasing vantage point towards Orkney. We drove west to an overnight camp on Dunnet Head, before a ferry from Thurso on the morrow. The quest for *three degrees* lay across the Pentland Firth.

# 30

# Orkney, the Sleeping Whales

## Mainland: Burwick to the city of Kirkwall

One of Orkney's resident writers, George Mackay Brown, once imagined the archipelago as whales asleep in the Pentland Firth, an apt description since most of the islands are humps of low ground, barely rising beyond the sea into the vastness of sky. One's first impression of Orkney, therefore, is misleading, since the *St Ola* ferry passes the highest island, Hoy, with its dramatic sea stack, The Old Man, 450 feet of sandstone and quartz. Behind this columnar welcome lie spectacular vertical cliffs a thousand feet in height, and the high muirs of Cuilags and Ward Hill, a nature reserve managed by the RSPB and famous for its seabird and raptor colonies. The ferry docks in Stromness, a quaint fishing harbour of narrow flagstoned streets and tiered houses which tumble down to the waterside.

Orkney – first impressions, The Old Man of Hoy.

*Three degrees* is on the west of 'mainland' Orkney, and I resumed the route on South Ronaldsay, at Burwick, by the pier which serves the passenger route from John O' Groats. The weather was sunny, but oh, so windy. Westerlies had been pulling at the islands for several days as the autumn equinox was imminent. Links with the Caithness coast were provided by views south to Duncansby Head, and east to the twin lights of Muckle Skerry, which we had seen clearly from the Scottish mainland. We headed into the wind, turned west for the South Ronaldsay coast, and looked across to the nearby whale of Swona.

Orkney is a green and fertile land which has been tilled to the cliff edges for over 5,000 years by man. Cattle in particular are plentiful, though sheep, bere (the traditional barley) and potato production make the Orkney landscape a tapestry of field patterns and textures. Woodland is almost completely absent from the isles, and fence-posts are made of flags and barbed wire, with straining posts of concrete or driftwood. Cottage roofs are made of flagstones too, and stane dykes are ubiquitous.

Along the clifftop, we admired the fulmars hanging in the wind. It was late in the season and only buttercups and scabious remained in bloom. Golden plovers and lapwings rested in the close-cropped fields. We were surrounded by the sea and the sky. To the east was a bizarre view of a tanker's super-structure which appeared anchored above the horizon. An Orcadian had informed us that no oil had moved from the Occidental oil terminal on the island of Flotta in Scapa Flow since the Piper

Twites, the linnets of the North – *Orkney*.

Alpha disaster several weeks earlier, and the skippers had dropped anchor in safe anchorages to await developments. Under normal circumstances an average daily rate of 340,000 barrels, or fifteen per cent of the United Kingdom production, travels along the 128-mile pipeline from the Piper field in the North Sea. The terminal operates twenty-four hours a day, purifying and separating the mixture of crude oil and gas into the waiting supertankers for use in Europe and America. Flotta was chosen because of its natural deepwater harbour in Scapa Flow.

Moving Meg across the fields was difficult because of the high number of cattle present. In one field a persistent beast worried us greatly by her angry presence. Progress along the clifftops was much easier since the field invariably ended several yards before the edge, and a narrow strip of turf or maritime heath afforded a route. Crab carapaces littered the heathland, giving a crunch to our springy steps. Much of the rolling agricultural landscape has been reclaimed from muirland, and a vivid reminder of this came at the Nev above Sandwick, where a diagonal of colour separated the old and new landscapes.

Gannets patrolled the waters of Scapa Flow close to the cliffline, and we admired these gigantic hunters as they sliced the waters, plunging for fish from a great height. Eiders, or *dunters* to the Orcadians, waddled off the rock platforms into the surf, and dunlin and turnstone wheeled in unison over the waves. Along the clifftops, twites twittered from the barbed wire fences. Everything, animal, mineral or vegetable, suffered from the torment of the wind.

Somewhere along the route disaster struck, and I lost a camera lens. Somehow it slipped from its case, perhaps when I was climbing over the innumerable fences along the way. This upset me greatly, particularly since it was the most useful lens, and irreplaceable on Orkney. I sulked at Sandwick as I read a religious notice, and was advised by the same to take a gospel tract. This I did, and the wind blew it away before I had a chance to digest its contents — lens and liturgy lost at South Ronaldsay. A month later, the Northern Constabulary returned the lost property to me none the worse for its exposure to the Orkney elements!

We crossed a hill into the sweep of Widewall Bay, and overlooked the township of Herston and Hoxa Head. A fishing boat was tied to the salmon cages in the bay — fish farming is big business on Orkney, with most of the produce travelling south by refrigerated lorry to Billingsgate. An old mill caught our attention at Newbigging. Many mills remain in Orkney and they are invariably three-storey buildings, with the water-driven grinding wheels operating at the upper and central storeys. Some mills had a kiln at one end to dry the bere. Only one mill

Oat reaper,
St Margaret's Hope.

remains as a working unit, and sadly, the mill on our route was derelict. The tide was high, and no sand was exposed along the Oyce of Quindy. We entered the pretty village of St Margaret's Hope nestling in yet another natural inlet of Scapa Flow, and remarked on its similarity to the much larger Stromness. St Margaret's Hope is named after the arrival in the bay in the thirteenth century of Margaret, the child-maid of Norway. Unfortunately she lay dead, having failed to survive a terrible tempest in the North Sea, and the village name commemorates her dreams of becoming Queen of Norway, Scotland and England. Beyond St Margaret's Hope, oats were being cut by an old-fashioned cutter and binder, pulled by an old Massey Ferguson, two-a-penny in the islands. An ancient sat on the cutter with the blank expression of an old hand, although his eye did acknowledge our passing. A youth stacked the bundles into sixes to form stooks, to dry in the singing winds. Later they would be threshed and bruised, and fed to the cattle over winter.

Scapa Flow is 120 square miles of watery history enclosed by a circle of sleeping whales. Its strategic position, controlling the North Sea and the Atlantic, has been recognised over the centuries by the Vikings and the Kings of Scotland and Norway. Perhaps its most dramatic incidents took place during the two world wars. At the conclusion of the Great War in 1918, the German High Seas Fleet surrendered to the Royal Navy, and in November of that year seventy vessels were interned at Scapa Flow. There then followed months of political wrangling as the allies attempted to resolve the future of the *Hochseeflotte*. Ashamed of this, on Saturday 21st June 1919 the German

Blockship, Churchill
Barrier.

Commander-in-Chief ordered the secret scuttling of his entire
fleet, and, at a given signal, the captains opened the seacocks and
the fleet disappeared beneath the waters. Between the wars the
salvage operations on the German vessels provided much
employment for Orcadians!

North of St Margaret's Hope is a causeway named Churchill
Barrier No. 4, which links the islands of South Ronaldsay and
Burray. Further Churchill Barriers, Nos. 3, 2 and 1, link Burray,
Glimps Holm, and Lamb Holm to 'Mainland'. These barriers
were constructed between 1940 and 1944 by the civil
engineering company Balfour Beatty, with the assistance of
Italian prisoners of war. During the two world wars Scapa Flow
had been the major British base of the home fleet, and in order
to defend its many entrances tramp steamers had been
purposely scuttled in strategic entrances as blockships, to prevent
entry by German submarines. Because of the fierce tidal rips
through Scapa Flow, and the presence of blockships, cables and
nets, the naval base was generally considered to be well defended
at the start of World War Two.

The war was barely six weeks old, though, when a daring
young German submariner named Lt Prien pierced the defences
through Holm Sound. He prowled around Scapa Flow,

torpedoed *HMS Royal Oak* anchored on *three degrees* in Scapa Bay, and escaped back into the North Sea. The huge 31,200-ton, 624-foot battleship sank with major loss of life, 833 men, and the British government was alerted to the inadequacy of the defences. As a consequence, Churchill ordered the construction of the barriers to protect its eastern entrances. It was a major civil engineering feat, combating the fast tides and Atlantic gales of Orkney by the use of overhead cableways to dump the materials in the channels. Half a million cubic yards of quarried rock and 300,000 tons of concrete eventually sealed the sounds, and provided protection for the fleet and the thousands of servicemen stationed on Orkney. It has made the southern isles much more accessible, for the causeways provide road access between 'Mainland' and South Ronaldsay.

The tiny islet of Lamb Holm, between Churchill Barriers 1 and 2, is home to another remarkable wartime engineering feat — a small chapel which was built by Italian prisoners. We marvelled at the beautiful and intricate workmanship, which disguised the chapel's Nissen hut skeleton. The work was supervised by P.O.W. Signor Chiocchetti who belonged to the high Dolomites of Italy, another world away from the bleak windswept prison of Lamb Holm.

I resumed my walk beyond the village of St Mary's into an ever-strengthening gale, and had to battle my way along the clifftop towards Scapa Bay. Seventeen ships were at anchor in Scapa Flow, including eight German warships, the largest and most ironic German presence in these waters for over seventy years. Amongst their number was the frigate *Karlsruhe*, a namesake of one of the *Hochseeflotte* which was scuttled in 1919! Apparently NATO were conducting an 'attack' on Norway, and the German Section had manoeuvred into Scapa Flow to escape the rigours of the Atlantic. An oil support vessel sporting a Norwegian flag sailed by, possibly on its way to help defend Norway.

Further sinister events occurred as we passed the corpses of a gannet and a common seal. The gannet was a juvenile of two or three years, easily recognisable by the smaller amount of white on its plumage. The cause of its death was a mystery. Not so with the common seal, for an epidemic of a distemper virus was sweeping the North Sea population, and dead seals were littering Orkney's beaches. We counted thirteen during our stay. Meg was given a booster inoculation and was kept off the beaches as far as practicable. It was sad to see the seals, the *selchies* of Scottish folklore, ripped apart by the gulls. Death is part of nature's cycle, and the Orkney fishermen were arguing that this was nature's method of culling the high seal population, since culls had been prohibited by the government. Animals are not the only things to die, and I passed a graveyard of old agricultural

Even a large female
hen harrier seemed
troubled by the gale
— *Scapa Flow*.

implements close by a skeleton of a mill wheel. Straining posts along here were made from an old ship's keel. I spied a buoy offshore at Haddieweel marking the wargrave of *HMS Royal Oak*.

It was a strength-sapping experience along the clifftops of Holm Parish, through clumps of the high heather and turfs of Gaitnip Hill, and against the screaming wind. At one point, a *bonxie* hung in the wind much like a buzzard would, motionless and sinister. A wren dived for cover amidst the clumps. It was difficult to reconcile the small brown speck of life with the angry elements surrounding it. Even a large female hen harrier seemed troubled but ravens simply played with the gale. Hen harriers are uncommon raptors in mainland Britain, but on Orkney their distinctive flight, all wings and tail, is commonplace. Scapa Bay is headed by a sandy sweep, capped by Scapa distillery. A pier interrupted our sightline from the south, from which a pilot-boat sped away, and cut through the wind and sea with arrogance.

Scapa Bay is but a mile from Orkney's capital, the city of Kirkwall, and the sandy bay is popular with the town's 7,000 residents. Kirkwall is situated on an isthmus between two bays, and the sea is ever-present. It may be the only town in Britain with a roadsign which warns of *otters crossing*. Dominating the town is the twelfth-century St Magnus cathedral, and its name in old Norse means 'Kirk bay'. In the early twelfth century Orkney was ruled by two rival Earls, one of whom, Earl Magnus Erlendsson, was murdered by his jealous cousin, Earl Hakon. Before long his grave was said to possess healing powers, and pilgrims came to visit his grave at Birsay, until his remains were transferred to St Olaf's Kirk in Kirkwall. In 1137, Earl Magnus's nephew, Rognvald Kolsson, decided to build a magnificent stone

Kirkwall skyline.

minster to commemorate his uncle, and to raise political support for his rule. Work began simultaneously on the cathedral and the Bishop's Palace opposite, such that Kirkwall became a prestigious centre of power from the twelfth century. When King Haakan of Norway was defeated by the Scots in 1263 at the Battle of Largs, he retired to Orkney, became ill and died in the Bishop's Palace. Another palace, the Earl's Palace, was built nearby in 1600 by Earl Stewart. A curious tradition still survives in Kirkwall which derives from the split between Church and State. Kirkwall Castle was completed in 1380 by Earl Henry St Clair, which led to geat rivalry between the Earldom and the Bishops. Every Christmas and Hogmanay, a game called the *Ba'* is held in the streets of Kirkwall between the *Uppies* (the Bishop's men) and the *Doonies* (the Earl's men). This rugby-like spectacle is ideally suited to the narrow, flagged streets of the Kirkwall conservation area! Another curious tradition is the pre-nuptual male celebrations of wandering almost naked through the town, with the groom covered in black, beating drums and consuming alcohol! We witnessed wedding celebrations in a pickup truck, from which the shouts of the participants and the beating of oil drums echoed through the capital all afternoon.

Kirkwall pier was busy with vessels of all shapes and sizes. One frontage was occupied by the Orkney Islands Shipping Company, berths for the *Islander* and *Orcadia,* ships which serve the island communities. Norwegian and German vessels were docked as well, providing a modern link with the North Sea and the Baltic, which has been a feature of Kirkwall for centuries. Beyond the Wide Firth lay the Parish of Rendall and the island of Rousay, northward on *three degrees.*

# 31

# Meg Sings to the Selchies

## The Parish of Rendall

The Parish of Rendall lies on the north-east mainland, by the waters of Wide Firth, a natural harbour formed by the islands of Mainland, Gairsay and Shapinsay. *Three degrees* lies barely offshore, on the eastern coastline of Rendall. To the west lie the high muirs of Evie, Burgar Hill and Mid Hill. Burgar Hill boasts a modern three-megawatt windmill, the world's most powerful aero-generator, whose column stands forty-five feet above the summit of the hill, and which cost £10 million to build. Its twin blades span sixty feet, and visitors must walk directly beneath these whilst they sear through the air with a spectacular and frightening noise. There is a RSPB hide next to the site, and we had gone to watch a red-throated diver chick on the small lochan. In winter the wind speeds on Burgar Hill can exceed 100 mph, but the 3MW generator is designed to generate electricity only in moderate winds, and to shut down under inclement weather. The thing actually stopped whilst we were present, and it screamed to a halt quickly and efficiently by the use of flaps on its gigantic blades. It dwarfs its two smaller neighbours, experimental prototypes, is capable of generating electricity for up to 2,000 homes, and is linked to the national grid by a 28-mile submarine cable. A visitor centre on the site explains all,

The 3 MW aero-generator, Burgar Hill.

and one is left contemplating the trade-offs which must be made in all forms of energy generation. Burgar Hill's generator, rather than being intrusive, very quickly became a familiar landmark, if somewhat incongruous for a birdwatching hide. In order to be commercially viable, however, generators need to be tripped along the hillsides, ridges or levées, as in California or Holland, and it is on this scale that they cause a major aesthetic problem. Set against fossil fuel generators with the resultant acid rain, and nuclear reactors with waste disposal problems, energy generation remains a difficult issue to resolve.

Our route at Rendall took us along the narrow lanes through freshly cut fields of stooks which contrasted dramatically with the huge round bales clothed in black plastic. Orkney is all contrast, from stooks to polythene, heather to leys, and sea to sky. A fearsome wind still swept the landscape, and we set off from the kennels and cattery at Hoversta to a cacophony of dogs. 'Don't worry about the dogs — they won't touch you!' shouted a friendly woman leaning on the gate. 'Call in for a cup of tea after your walk, and watch out for the bull in the next field!' She retreated from the wind, and became a pied piper as the dogs followed her lead.

Sure enough, a big Hereford bull ruled the next field. They're acknowledged to be placid beasts, but try telling that to Kate or Meg. Cattle were everywhere to landward. Beef cattle production plays an important role in Orkney's economy, with over 25,000 cattle shipped south annually. Twice as many sheep leave each year, and milk production currently stands at 16 million litres per annum, much being used in the production of Orkney cheese. The cattle boat to the mainland is the aptly named *Livestock Express*! We proceeded behind the protection of a barbed wire fence and gained the coastline.

A carpet of ochre seaweed lay over the rocks in such pretty patterns that *selchies* were suspected of frequenting the shore. We walked over a tailor's floor of marine material. Filaments of algae, thread for *selchies'* clothes, lay amongst the fawns, oranges and deep browns of seaweed cloths. Out to sea, eiders and mergansers bobbed like corks. Waders winged by on the wind, curlew, snipe, oystercatcher, redshank, turnstone, golden plover and peewit. It was bleak, and a heron battled against the fray and shrieked into the wind.

Shapinsay was barely visible through the murk, across Wide Firth. The turrets of Balfour Castle on Shapinsay seemed a defiant outpost against sea and weather. Gairsay was closer at hand and without doubt a sleeping whale. A ruined kirkyard in the Bay of Hinderayre was yet another reminder of Scotland's history of rural depopulation, its gravestones mainly dating from the mid-nineteenth century, and encrusted with green lichens. A broch site nearby was a mere grassy mound around which a *bonxie* circled. Shortly afterwards we received definitive proof that the *selchies* were at large, by Meg who ran on ahead and howled out to sea.

We walked as far as the doocot at Rendall, which was built in 1648 to a beehive design, the only one of this type on Orkney. A plaque told of the history of dovecotes in Scotland and Orkney. Apparently the Normans introduced dovecotes to England, and they were established in Scotland by the sixteenth century. They have great antiquity, however, and holes at Skara Brae on Orkney, a 5,000-year-old Stone Age settlement, older than the Pyramids, have been suspected of being man-made dove nesting holes. Until turnips were introduced to Scotland from Sweden in the eighteenth century, doves provided winter food. Dove dung is rich in potassium nitrate, and was even mixed with black earth and sulphur to make gunpowder! This beehive full of doves was remarkable, and its interior reeked of dung. Rats were prevented from climbing the exterior walls by a clever series of courses, though the pigeons flapped crazily out when we human intruders entered.

Three hours had passed since we had left the kennels, and on our return we felt in need of the promised cup of tea. The Cooks made us welcome, and conversation with Mike and Heather was easy. They had moved from Portsmouth in the deep south to Orkney two years before, to begin their first kennel business. Mike managed the animals, whilst Heather's job as a community nurse reduced the risks inherent in a new enterprise. Baby Thomas had just arrived, and took his place among their four dogs and a cat. We spoke of their settling, of the things that they missed, and the good life of Orkney. They were both Morris dancers, with Portsmouth sides, and missed the socialising of English pubs and beer. Many English people have settled in Orkney, and generally have fitted in well. Only those without work and skills have been resented. It is easy to idealise island life, which is a far cry from the practicalities of a difficult existence. Orcadians have mixed blood, and this is a positive factor in their survival and ability to adapt. The English, or mainland Scots for that matter, are known as *ferry loopers* and are teased but respected. We detected some parochial attitudes within the archipelago. Notable comments were made to us regarding the strangely behaved *Dons* of Westray, for example, a supposedly excitable race, following the mixing of Norse blood with the Spanish survivors of the wrecked Armada. For our part, we received nothing but kindness and politeness on Westray, or any other island, and decided that impressions are largely in the eye of the beholder.

Mike and Heather are warm folk, and we ended by staying three nights, and remain friends to this day. There is more to *three degrees* than just a walk.

# 32

# The Queen of the Isles and the Ship of Death

## Rousay

The equinox gales continued. We clambered aboard M.V. *Eynhallow,* the ferryboat which serves the cluster of islands around Rousay, Wyre and Egilsay. It was Sunday, and we had few fellow passengers — a couple and their baby going to a family reunion, and a Yorkshire tyke who was heading for work on a Rousay fish farm. Our crossing was lumpy, but brief, and inside half an hour we were climbing up the hill away from the pier and the fish processing co-operative. To begin with we headed west, to explore the archaeology of the Midhowe chambered cairn. The road contours Rousay along its south shore at around 120 feet, and gives good views across Wyre Sound to the tiny island of Wyre, across Eynhallow Sound to the even smaller isle of Eynhallow and the mainland hills of Evie. The Burgar Hill 3MW monster was dominant.

The Hills of Hoy.

At Trumland House we took a detour into its woodland policies, and entered among its superb contorted and squat sycamore, laburnum, and elder. Fuschias formed thickets and hedges, an oddity to be sure, the pink bells swaying to the creak of the woodland. A small burn tumbled through the wood, and the resultant tangle of undergrowth and noise was unique on Orkney. Trumland House, Scots baronial in style, was empty, no doubt its upkeep being too expensive for its laird.

The three islands hold almost 200 archaeological and historical sites, a staggering tapestry revealing 5,000 years of settlement. Mindful of how short our time on the island was, we passed by the two chambered cairns of Taversoe Tuick and Blackhammer. We had planned an optimistically long walk west to Midhowe, then through the island's centre by the twin lochs of Muckle and Peerie Waters, returning by the east coast to overlook Rousay Sound. Fortunately the local minister stopped and gave us a lift for three miles along the road, which saved us an hour and took away the pressure of time. He was studying for the ministry, out of Aberdeen University, and was enjoying his stay on Rousay. A local inhabitant later told us that he was a popular figure and would be much missed. The minister informed us that half of Rousay's 240 people were incomers, and that there had been some friction caused by land feuds. By contrast, only one Orcadian remained on Egilsay, but the island was considered too small and remote by Orcadians, so there had been no problems with *ferry loopers*. We were grateful for the lift, and wished our benefactor well with his studies, and ran down the hill towards the shore and Midhowe, the *ship of death*.

It is not difficult to imagine Midhowe, the largest known stalled chambered cairn, as a *ship of death*. Built around 3,500 BC, it is now protected from Orkney's ceaseless elements by its own hangar, and a viewing platform has been constructed over the tomb. Each of the twenty-five burial compartments were enclosed with stone slabs along a 69-foot long central chamber, the tombs having been used for many generations, and the entrance deliberately blocked after the last burial. Its construction was exquisite, a massive hump of drystane technology in the shape of a vessel, covering the bones of oxen, sheep, red deer, pigs and birds and the bones and souls of the farmers and hunters of 5,000 years ago. Midhowe is a moving place. Whilst visiting this and the other archaeological masterpieces of Orkney — Skara Brae, the Ring of Brodgar, and the Maeshowe chambered tomb — we felt closer to our ancestors than ever we do on mainland Britain. Adjacent to the chambered cairn is Midhowe Broch, a well-preserved Iron Age tower from the first century, of intricate passageways and chambers, an impregnable fortress built by a mysterious people. Stone is used to create household details such as shelving, recesses and fire pits. Skara Brae, a Stone Age village preserved by a freak sandstorm, has even a drainage system, beds and cupboards, all made from stone!

We turned south-east and headed along the Westness Walk, and strolled through centuries of history from the Stone Age at Midhowe, the Iron Age of the broch, and a Viking cemetery at Moa Ness. Ruined farmhouses and a kirkyard were more recent, but medieval in origin. Skail Farm had a small ruined round tower which we guessed must have been a kiln or an oven. A friendly farmer's wife at Westness gave us much information, relating the composition of the island's population. As she lifted the potatoes, she spoke sadly about the plight of the seals, as her husband, who shepherds Eynhallow, had found many carcasses on the island.

We trekked across the centre of the island, climbing 300 feet or so onto a central plateau, where lay the Muckle (big) and Peerie (small) waters. These were windswept lochs with long striations of foam straggling the surface led by the wind. We huddled behind a concrete dam for some coffee and respite. A wee jack snipe, the first of the winter, struggled away. They are tiny birds and fly only as a last resort when they are about to be trodden upon, with a direct, silent flight. Their behaviour makes them difficult to spot, and it amazes me that they are able to cross the North Sea, for they breed in Scandinavia and Russia. It would not be long before other winter visitors arrived from the north, the winter thrushes of fieldfares and redwings. Berries were ripe in the heather, and already the bird droppings on the path were stained purple. We ran out of track and bounced our way across peat hags and rough heather clumps for only a mile, but it seemed like an eternity.

At last we began to pass active peat workings, with plastic sacks, barrows and peat-cutting tools lending an aspect of toil to the scene. This was a good sign, for surely a track was nearby. The burn ran brown with the peat, and a delicious scent mingled faintly in our nostrils, of the wind, the water, the peat and the whisky. Otter tracks were spotted in the mud, the nearest we got to one — they are commoner on some islands than others. We rounded a corner, and beyond Kierfea Hill lay Westray, the ultimate goal of my *third degree* quest. This evoked a strange sensation; an expectation, a thrill.

We turned southward and overlooked Egilsay. St Magnus's church was a prominent feature because of its distinctive round tower. It was built by the Norse settlers, and fell into disuse in the mid-nineteenth century. Here the two Earls, Hakan and Magnus, had faced each other, leading to Magnus's martyrdom. Their meeting had been arranged for the purposes of reconciliation, but Hakan the unscrupulous tricked Magnus and cleaved his skull with an axe. More bloodthirsty tales are told in

Otter tracks were
spotted in the mud
– *Rousay.*

the epic *Orkneyinga Saga,* the history of the Earls of Orkney, essential reading for a visit to the islands. Herein are tales of *Thorfinn Skull-Splitter, Eirik Blood-Axe, Sigmund Fish-Hook, and King Magnus Bare-legs,* to name but a few.

Small industries prospered on east Rousay, including market gardening and a fish hatchery. The fish hatchery utilises the Suso burn, and is operated by the brothers Bruce and Hugh Mainland who buy in 70,000 salmon eggs each year from Argyll. When the eggs hatch, feeding occurs automatically, once a minute, over a twenty-hour day, which is achieved with artificial light. Salmon farming is big business on Orkney and in 1986 produced 237 tons of salmon, worth nearly £1 million. Over 300 fish farms now exist in Scotland, despite major concerns over the pollution that they create and their visual impact. Orkney farms which we saw seemed less offensive, perhaps because of their archipelagic setting. Where inlets and bays are so numerous, the loss of· a few to fish farms seemed less intrusive than on the Scottish mainland.

Indeed, fishing is an important industry to *third degree* Scotland, from the fishing fleet of Fife, to the salmon nets of Spey Bay; the salmon farms off No. 1 Barrier and Rousay, and the fish processing co-operatives of Rousay and Westray. On Westray, we would befriend a fisherman, and learn much about the harsh ways of the sea.

# 33 Aboard K440 *The Wings of the Morning*

## The North Sound, Sound of Faray, Westray Firth and Papa Sound

The breaker battered
our boats, cracked
in sleet-storm our two
sisters, our ships.
Curling, the killer-wave
crushed lives, the crew
endured: the undaunted
Earl's story won't die.

Earl Rognvald, *Orkneyinga Saga*

By any standards, the crew of *Wings of the Morning,* one of Westray's five lobster and crab boats, is a hard-working one. We loaded several boxes of fish bait, and left Pierowall harbour early one morning just after six, to catch the tides, and only returned to harbour over twelve hours later. Edwin Groat the skipper, and his crew Wilbert and trainee Duncan, put in some eighty

Pierowall harbour –
*Wings of the Morning* is
the last boat.

196

Edwin Groat– skipper,
*Wings of the Morning.*

hours of work each week around the waters of the northern isles of Orkney. It takes a force eight gale to confine the boat to harbour, and even when the winds blow hard there may be some hope for the fishing in coveted sheltered spots in the sounds between the isles. Danger is ever-present, and Edwin related the story of a recent fatality on a similar vessel when a deckhand had become entangled in the creel lines, held by their awful drag and lost beneath the waters. Edwin's lines utilise 240 fathoms of line, with twenty creels set at twelve-fathom intervals. Against this kind of weight, the boy hadn't stood a chance, and Edwin shrugged his shoulders, heavy with realism. His son works on a deep-sea fishing boat out of Westray, and the Orkney fisherfolk know that the fertile sea is never slow to reclaim some of her productivity.

We fished the waters of *three degrees* off Westray in Edwin's fifteen-year-old ferro-concrete lobster boat — built in Bristol. His charge was named after verses of Psalm 139, and Edwin proudly showed us the text in the bible he carried in the cabin: 'If I take the wings of the morning, and dwell in the uppermost parts of the sea; Even there shall thy hand lead me, and thy right hand shall hold me'.

She was kitted out with modern echo-sounding gear. Edwin freely confessed that the electronic equipment was beyond his ken. Kate and I paid for our passage by correcting the Decca navigator which had been malfunctioning for some time. 'Even the representative didnae understand it . . .,' said Edwin with a twinkle in his eye. 'Jist leave it to the youngsters the man said — they'll work it oot!' Talking with Edwin was a pleasure for he was a fund of local knowledge. We sailed by Faray and he told us that the small island was owned by the Church of Scotland, and that the tenant farmer spent six weeks of the year living on the isle, lambing its 700 sheep. We sailed by Eday and he told us of Norfolk settlers who had done much to improve the farmland and the wildlife. Orkney voles had been introduced onto the headland in an effort to attract harriers and owls. He spoke of the Eday folk as *scarfs* (cormorants or shags), and told us that all islanders had familiar names after the seabirds. Westray folk were known as *acks* (auks).

Edwin has more than a touch of the Viking in his blood, and was happy to listen to and translate a Norwegian shipping forecast for us. His radio conversations with the skipper of another Westray boat were almost unintelligible. After a sail down North Sound, the fishermen began their hard work. During the course of the day they would haul in, inspect and re-bait some 400 creels, and be rewarded with sixty-seven lobsters. It was a bright, cheerful day with only a slight swell on the sea, yet not difficult to imagine the work under inclement conditions. Their teamwork was impeccable. Edwin operated the winch on the starboard beam of *Wings*, and brought the creels aboard. The skipper had a keen eye and could spot the bumper creels complete with pairs of lobsters whilst they were still submerged. Many creels were empty, and many contained the much less valuable brown crabs or *pattens*. Edwin cleared the creels and depended on Wilbert to re-bait and secure the fastenings. Duncan then neatly stacked the cages, aft. Edwin would then decide upon another area to fish, and Wilbert would *shoot the creels* over the beam as Duncan fed them to him. To move 400 of these creels in a day was heavy work, particularly the larger *Yankee parlour* creels, half as big again as the traditional design. Periods of sailing between fishing spots would be occupied by tidying the decks, repairing the creels, or placing rubber bands around the menacing pincers of the lobsters. This was done gingerly by Duncan who was a novice and was nipped for his inexperience more than once. Chores on the deck were accompanied by the crunching of carapaces underfoot. Progress was tricky, if not dangerous, because of the combination of the swell and the slippery bodies of fish, eels, and bait.

As their work proceeded, so *Wings of the Morning* gained in character. Lobsters, crabs, starfish, sea urchins, conger eels and octopuses joined the deck. Electric-blue lobsters stunned us with their beauty, and were placed carefully under damp hessian, to ensure their survival until the return to the processing plant at Pierowall. Crabs were neatly stacked in fish boxes. Octopuses

Lobster boat, Orkney.

were despised, as predators of lobsters, and rivals to the fishers. Edwin showed us the hollow shell of a lobster, with an octopus sharing the creel. Occasionally an octopus would escape the attentions of the crew because of the frenetic activity as the creels were hauled in and stacked. There was a bizarre sight as one climbed the cabin. It changed colour at will and instantaneously, merging with ease into its surroundings. Eventually it died and slopped to the deck with an ignominious *splat*.

I was curious to know how the different boats decided their fishing areas, and was somewhat surprised to learn that it was a free-for-all. 'Cut-throat' said Edwin, with another twinkle in his eye. Experience rather than the echo-sounder had taught him and the other skippers where to fish. They look for rocky shores where the lobsters live in holes on the seabed. Two or three lobsters off each line is considered reasonable fishing. Autumn was the lobster season, and they fished brown crabs in the spring and summer, 'and for anything that would go in the creels' in the winter. Edwin's catch would be stored live in the processing plant at Pierowall until the correct price could be obtained for the produce. In the evening I escorted the lobsters to their limbo, and realised the necessity of the rubber bands around their pincers. Sixty-seven territorial lobsters can do no damage to their fellow inmates once their weapons are bound. They would be shipped by refrigerated transport to markets in London and France. A new market had opened up recently for the green velvet crabs, and these travelled the length of Britain and France, to Spain.

Small crabs and lobsters less than eighty-five millimetres were returned to the sea. We caught one or two 'old boys' — barnacle-encrusted lobsters — many years old, which command a lesser price than the younger, more succulent crustaceans. Damaged lobsters were also less valuable, being less aesthetic for the high-class restaurants. Edwin treats his catch with care. Each electric-blue lobster was worth around an electric-blue fiver. One creel contained an enormous lobster claw, far bigger than our largest monster of the day, which prompted another twinkle and an old fisherman's adage, 'the one that got away!'

We fished Seal Skerry, we fished 'the Grither', and we fished *three degrees* off Westray. Edwin listened to my stories of *three degrees* with as much interest and amazement as we listened to him. He was a kind man and the boat fishing on *three degrees* meant much to me. Noup Head and Bow Head off the port beam were a far cry from that first wild night in the Undercliffs, yet the noise of the sea provided a common bond, a thread of *three degrees*.

# The Return of the Pinkfeet

## Westray

Our timing had been out for the trip to Westray, and in the end we resorted to a flight by a Loganair *Islander*. We even missed the scheduled flight, and went out on a charter run which brought the schoolchildren from Westray back to school in Kirkwall. Every month they are allowed home for a long weekend, and, aged fourteen onwards, become accustomed to the twelve-minute flight. Dave was the pilot of the intimate nine-seater aircraft. He had the air of a seasoned campaigner, and piloted our extremely turbulent flight in a friendly but efficient manner. Kate, Meg and I were his only passengers on the trip out. Meg was spared the prospect of wearing a muzzle only because Loganair's spare had not managed to return to Kirkwall from Wick that morning! I assured Dave that he would be relatively safe from our man-eating collie. I doubt if she enjoyed the flight though, for it was bumpy in the unpredictable manner of the skies, and must have been incomprehensible to a dog. We left Kirkwall and began to familiarise ourselves with the landscape, a mere two or three hundred feet above the islands, flying north over Inganess Bay and Hellier Holm, identified by its light. Shapinsay was easy to spot because of Balfour Castle and its parallel roads. To port lay Gairsay and the Rousay group,

Island life, Kirkwall airport.

including the distinctive St Magnus Kirk. We continued over
Eday, with its peat fields and London Airport (a grass
strip!). Eday was intensely agricultural, with neat, square fields. Over
North Sound, a tall ship sailed beneath us, all sail and elegance.
An Orkney tapestry is best seen from the air.

Dave took us safely in to the landing strip on Westray, a field
with an air-sock. Across Papa Sound lay Papa Westray (*Papay* to
the Orcadians), served by the world's shortest scheduled air
service, a Loganair flight between Westray and Papa Westray.
Apparently airline buffs the world over come to travel this 90-
second hop, which can be even shorter with a following wind!
Loganair's six *Islander* aircraft also fly more than 1,000 Air
Ambulance missions in the islands every year for the Scottish Air
Ambulance Service. We were two of Loganair's 300,000 annual
passengers and enjoyed our flight immensely.

Dot Groat met us and drove us a couple of miles down the
road to her home in Pierowall. She runs a bed and breakfast
business, whilst her husband is at sea. Their boy has followed his
father's calling to the sea, and she had just escorted her daughter
to the airport where Dave was taking her back to Kirkwall and
secondary school. She is a generous woman who troubled herself
on our behalf, and made us welcome on Westray.

As with Rousay, I took a *three degree* perambulation, rather
than the usual route from south to north. Pierowall is a semi-
circular sweep lining the semi-circular bay. On the north side is
the pier which accommodates the *Orcadia* and the Westray
fishing fleet. Westray's fish-processing co-operative and an old
fishing warehouse complete Pierowall's northern flank. Two or
three shops, a primary school, an hotel and a post office form
the backbone of the village itself. On the sands opposite the
Groats' house we admired bar-tailed godwits, sanderling and
dunlin. Behind Pierowall lies the Loch of Burness, the haunt of
wildfowl. Seven pinkfeet flew in, the first of the winter. A
solitary whooper swan graced the loch, possibly a summer
resident in these northern latitudes. Widgeon whistled over the
water. Satisfied with our birding, we headed south down the
'main' road, and passed haystacks and starlings. Old ploughs
plugged gaps in the fence lines as we wandered through the
pastures, admiring the muirs to the west. Two bulls eyeballed
each other across the road, much to the amusement of a
farmhand. At Gallowhill an inquisitive scan with my binoculars
along the horizon picked up a large 'raptor' head on, too large
for anything other than an eagle. When it turned through ninety
degrees, however, it gained a long neck and trailing feet, in
addition to its large upturned primaries. It was a crane, and we
sped over a couple of fields to investigate at closer quarters.
Fortunately it had landed by a small pool in a field corner, and
we took field notes for twenty minutes. A smoke-grey body was

superbly complemented by a black tail ruffle, and an elegant black and white neck. We were close enough to see its brick-red beak, yet managed to leave the vagrant in peace. I decided that the sighting was important enough to report to the RSPB's Orkney officer, Eric Meek, who told me as diplomatically as possible that it had been on Westray since July, but it was useful to know that it was still present!

We continued through the bere and pasture to the southern tip of *three degrees* on Westray, and looked southward to Rousay, where a muirburn plume trailed the sky — the sleeping whale was spouting. Once again St Magnus' church on Egilsay captured our attention. A rabbit was equally prominent on the rocks of the shore, amidst the rotting seaweed and a company of seals. We crossed the beach of Mae Sound, and the pockmarked turf, the work of burrowing rabbits. A ruined township at Nether House delayed us for some time, before we traversed Kirbist farm and climbed a wee glen on to the coastline. The farmland was Orcadian, of telephone wires singing in the wind, and redundant stone fence-posts in the fields like miniature nineteenth-century henges.

Westray's western coastline is spectacular. Two hundred-foot cliffs with arches and caves form a ten-mile tumult of waves. Fulmars hang in the wind, and in the breeding season the RSPB reserve of Noup Head at the north-west tip of Westray houses 40,000 guillemots and 25,000 kittywakes. We skipped along the short sea turf, looking for mushrooms, which were both enormous and delicious, and enjoyed the sparkle of Noup Head light in the sun. It was built in 1898, with some publicity, for it was the first light to utilise a system of mercury flotation for the revolving light carriage. It became automatic in 1964. Hundreds and hundreds of rabbits, many of them black, were responsible for our easy passage across the close-cropped turf. Beneath us, the sea crashed into a recess known as Gentleman's Cave, which was a place of refuge for the Jacobite Orcadian lairds in the '45. Tradition has it that it is linked by a subterranean passage to Noltland Castle, over two miles distant. Noltland is an airy ruin, full of sweeping steps and spiral staircases, built in the sixteenth century by Gilbert Balfour, a counsellor of Mary Queen of Scots.

At Big Geos we cut inland, overlooked Noltland Castle, and headed for the sounds and wave-cut platforms of Grobust. Muck-spreading filled the air with interest. Grobust has rabbits, dunes and a myriad of dykes built at right angles to the shore. These are used after the winter storms have delivered a harvest of kelp from the sea. Islanders hang the kelp over the dykes to dry, and sell the seaweed to alginate companies who use the substance in the manufacture of such products as toothpaste and ice cream. Most traditional crofters will spread seaweed on their land, for the weed is rich in phosphates. These crofters are continuing a tradition of seaweed harvest that has existed for centuries. During the Napoleonic wars it was used for its phosphate content in the manufacture of gunpowder. On North Ronaldsay, the most northerly of the Orkney isles (east of *three degrees*), an ancient breed of sheep grazes the shoreline and eats the stuff!

We continued northward into the failing light. Storm clouds were building overhead, and spectacular shafts pierced the sky to illuminate Noup Head. Paternoster lochans interspersed some cairns on the coastline. Dunlin fed at one lochan. Beyond the ruined house of Breck we realised our objective, the end of *third degree* Britain, Bow Head of Westray. Crashing waves, and the scratch of rabbits' claws over the rocks kept our senses alert. Now it was possible to view Noup Head through the sea arches to the west, and Mull Head on Papay to the east. To the north lay a swell beneath an angry sky, full of skeins of pinkfeet. In Papa Sound a collie dog on a lobster boat frantically ran fore and aft, barking furiously. More *selchies*? A pair of short-eared owls hunted over the farmland. We were over 600 miles from our starting point and Meg lay down and curled in a ball, as if to emphasise the point!

Shags flew along the shore. Large, Atlantic grey seals played in the surf. Above us were the familiar winter calls, the *wink, wink* of the wild geese. They were coming in on *three degrees* and we shared their songline.